NARCISSISTIC AND
COVERT EMOTIONAL ABUSE
2

*Recovery for Survivors of Childhood
Emotional Abuse*

By Diana Macey

Table of Contents

INTRODUCTION

This book is a follow-up from *Narcissistic Mothers and Covert Emotional Abuse*, a book about my covert-narcissistic mother and dysfunctional family of origin, and about my journey from being a victim to a survivor of childhood narcissistic abuse.

As a survivor I worked hard towards recovery. I went back and faced the painful details of the covert abuse I went through, and understood the effect it had on me in adulthood. I had a clear understanding of the damage done and how I should deal with it. Recovery was about using acceptance, compassion and self-love to heal the negativity, the shame and the self-loathing I had carried since childhood.

THE ISSUES I HAD MANAGED TO DEAL WITH

At this stage I'd had no contact with my family of origin for years. I was no longer suffering from depression or having self-destructive thoughts, and I was being increasingly positive about myself and my everyday life.

As a survivor I had no doubts about no contact, nor any feelings of obligation towards my narcissistic parent. I had managed to deal with my feelings of self-loathing and self-blame. I could handle the emotional flashbacks to a large degree and no longer felt I had to justify my existence.

THE REMAINING ISSUES

As a survivor I still had much anger about growing up in the toxic environment of my dysfunctional family of origin. As the hippocampus in my brain continued recovering, more memories kept surfacing, and I could not help thinking about what happened to me every day.

My mind kept going back to explore the damage, as well as trying to anticipate danger in the future. I had a very strong reaction of anger towards toxic people in general, as well as still experiencing anxiety and emotional dysregulation.

Part of this was, of course, due to the Complex PTSD children of narcissistic parents experience as a result of growing up in a family where the atmosphere is detrimental to their development and wellbeing.

Social anxiety was still an issue, or at least certain aspects of it. When I was alone I felt the full benefit of the recovery process. I could concentrate, enjoy activities, learn new things, and I felt quite content in general. The presence of others, however, often brought on the very familiar sensation of withdrawing mentally, as well as the physical reaction of becoming tense without any obvious reasons for it.

This sensation was triggered when the encounter was unexpected. It felt like I was reacting, despite my efforts to remain calm, and I often went into a familiar 'shrunken' mental state. This appeared to be a C-PTSD issue as well.

Such unhealthy reactions were well-entrenched in my brain and they could be triggered at certain times, especially in times of prolonged stress. If I became preoccupied and neglected to make a conscious effort to stay well, I went back to the childhood state of low anxiety, mixed with feelings of shame about the past and dread about the future. It was the state my brain was in for decades, and it was hard to override this early negative conditioning. This state was not a memory I could process nor something I could get rid of by crying.

The good news was that these episodes were now much shorter because I had the mental tools to deal with them. I could process any surfacing memories, acknowledge my authentic feelings, and understand that my worth as a person was not affected by my history, current circumstances, nor by the opinions of others.

Still, dealing with such episodes was hard work each time. It was energy draining. It happened less and less but it persisted, and it hindered my recovery.

So, even though I considered myself a survivor, the childhood abuse I grew up with was still an obstacle to living my life well, and I was not sure how to progress from there.

COPING WITH MY REMAINING ISSUES

For a while I was tempted to believe that this was as good as it was going to get, and that was fine. I no longer had suicidal thoughts, and I was having good experiences that made life worth living. I assumed that the injuries I had were too great for me to become a fully functioning human being.

That was not the case, of course. As a survivor I recognised that this was the way of thinking my narcissistic mother had instilled in me very early on. I was falling back into her insinuations that there was something inherently wrong with me that could not be fixed.

And if you have had the same thoughts, that is because of the gaslighting you have been through too.

As a survivor I was able and willing to look further for solutions. I kept on researching and trying different techniques to resolve the issues I was experiencing. Knowledge was what had helped me recover so far, and more knowledge was needed to get me to the next level. It was simply another stage of recovery that required different skills.

The best sources of information I found were psychologists and therapists who were once victims of narcissistic abuse themselves. Likewise, the online community of abuse survivors gave me a great deal of help and strength.

And, most importantly, as a survivor of narcissistic abuse I had experienced that amazing feeling of high spirits and ease that comes with unconditional self-love. It is a feeling of contentment and warm self-regard, a source of energy and comfort. That feeling had made all the effort worth it. If I could get that far, I could get further.

This book is about going from surviving to thriving, and about what I learned along the way.

PART I: Why Surviving is not Thriving

First let us start with a question: I knew I was not thriving at this stage, but how? And why?

I will give examples of some of the issues I was facing. One of them was the way I reacted to toxic people. Despite my progress in recovering, I was not reacting like a mentally healthy individual.

Examples:

As with anyone raised by a narcissist, I used to be an easy meal for users and abusers. Certain predatory types go after people with no self-esteem because such people are likely to give up their possessions and resources as well as their beliefs and values.

During my last depressive episode one of my neighbours made her way into my life. The way she operated was by using pretence and flattery – some people with this agenda use exaggerated compliments to get what they want.

While I was struggling with my mental health she used me to look after her kids, make birthday cakes and dinners for her husband, and many other small favours which took time and effort. Incidentally, she did nothing to return these favours. Of course it was my need to please that enabled her behaviour, and she took advantage because she could.

Toxic people are hard to get rid of and getting her out of my life was quite a challenge. When I pulled away, this person started ignoring me and focused her attention on my husband and the things he could do for her.

Yes, I know, she was not that bad compared to some of the predators out there. But this is not about her, it is about my reaction to her. She was a small-time user and not a real danger, and none of the above should have become a major issue for me. But it did. Ultimately, I had a severely angry reaction every time I caught a glimpse of her, and I could not avoid encountering her from time to time.

Encountering that kind of behaviour is unavoidable in life, and having the skill to ignore or cope with such people is necessary. I knew that well, yet I was affected badly each time I saw her. My heart would beat faster and I felt overwhelming anger.

This anger was the aftermath of a long history of abuse. It was the realisation that, so many times before, people like her had managed to use me and bring me down, emotionally and physically. Exhaustion and mental fatigue are common consequences of childhood narcissistic abuse. Another one is becoming a target for other abusers.

Clearly my anger was not only about my neighbour, and my overreaction was not a good thing. The only positive aspect I could find was the fact I was angry at her and not at myself.

I had an even worse reaction to another person who came to the neighbourhood. The first time we met he asked too many questions, and that alarmed me. He was standing way too close and he appeared to be trying to find out as much as he could about me and my husband, without saying anything about himself. I sensed something was wrong and my intuition was right. It turned out he was a manipulator who used lies to turn neighbours against each other for his own gain.

Similarly, it resulted in my reacting to his presence with every fibre of my body. I was angry he existed. Just a glance over the fence was enough to stir my anger. My state of mind was fight, fight, fight, but there was nothing to fight with physically.

At one stage I could not help but get the shakes each time I drove past his place. It was very unsettling. I felt I could jump on his throat if I had to. Of course, part of me was able to understand how unhelpful and ridiculous this emotional experience was. I knew I was having an overreaction, and the underlying sentiment behind it was: 'Do not let another toxic person use you. Not another one! Not another toxic person in my life!'

WHAT WAS GOING ON

I figured that the 'freeze' reaction I used to have when encountering such people in the past had turned into a 'fight' reaction. My knowledge of narcissistic abuse had turned into an anger against any predatory people I encountered.

This anger was taking my time and my energy. It was my heart that was beating faster, not the hearts of the two toxic people I mentioned. They didn't care. Also, it meant that these people had a hold over my state of mind and could make me upset the same way my narcissistic mother could.

Most of the anger appeared to come from the reactive animal part of my brain. It was as if I was still caught in the tense toxic atmosphere of my family, but this time I was prepared to fight like never before. The frontal lobe was not quite able to override that primal instinct and reactiveness.

It was a very new experience for me, being so ready to punch someone in the face. I was mature enough not to act on it, but undeniably there was a new set of reactions being activated in response to old threats. Somehow I had switched from freeze to fight, but it was like jumping from the fire back into the frying pan.

Thriving, as far as I understood, was about not being affected by narcissists and other toxic people, not even giving them a second thought. Not being affected at all. So, none of this was good. Overreacting was not helpful to my healing. The whole idea of healing was to have strong boundaries and to cope with life better, and this was not exactly happening.

The question, of course, was how to get there?

LOOKING FOR SOLUTIONS

It took some deep thinking, but eventually I did find the answer to this specific reaction and how to deal with it.

I realised that the anger I was feeling was so persistent and so overwhelming that it was clearly out of proportion to the deeds of the offenders. I was in such a turmoil, the source had to be much closer to home.

And it was. The anger directed towards these two toxic people was masking the fact I was still angry at myself. And I worked out why. I knew what these two individuals were like from the very start, but I ignored my good sense and my intuition. As a survivor I had the knowledge as well as the instinct to know better, but I ignored both and behaved as a victim yet again.

I felt upset because I had betrayed myself, but this time I projected the anger outwards instead of blaming myself. This, I thought, was an improvement, but it was not. I was not dealing with the problem and I was not dealing with my anger.

And, sure enough, the moment I understood what the issue was I was able to deal with it.

Self-abandonment is the worst damage done by the narcissistic abuser; as a survivor I know this well. And this was exactly it – I was angry at myself because I had failed to react the way I knew I should have during my encounters with these people.

With my first neighbour, there were many times I noticed her pretence and deceit over the years, yet I let her use me. 'Isn't it great that children like you for who you are?' – this was a comment she made when she left her children with me for a whole day. Even in the worst of my depression I knew this was complete nonsense, yet I overrode my good sense because I was not functioning like a healthy person. This was exactly what I used to do as a child and even as an adult – I overrode my senses and let my narcissistic mother manipulate me.

For example, what I wanted to do, and what I should have done with the second neighbour, was to say, 'You are standing way too close to me and please stop asking questions', and I should have said it in an even and polite tone. Then I should have politely excused myself and got rid of him without giving any information about myself.

This was what I should have done; as a survivor I knew that. And I was angry because I didn´t do that. I was attacking myself for acting as a victim but in a less obvious and direct fashion than I had in the past.

We survivors have good intuition and good sense, and this is how we have made it so far. Doubting this is a big part of the narcissistic damage to our identities. We end up destroying ourselves in the same way the narcissistic parent did.

FINDING THE REAL PROBLEM

To start with, I was as honest as I could be. I had superficially directed the problem away from myself, and this was something similar to what a narcissist does – directing the anger they have to an outside target in order to shift the blame away from themselves.

Narcissists project anger because it appears to work – one does not bash oneself but somebody else. This kind of reaction is not a solution, because the anger is only superficially displaced and it does not deal with the root of the problem.

Sure enough, my anger with the persons in the examples was not subsiding that way. I had to take another approach. What I had to do was face my failure to protect myself and examine the self-blame that I was feeling. I did that, and I accepted that I had made the old mistakes yet again. Then I employed all the compassion I could muster. Yes, I had failed again, but that was okay. Recovery is a process and compassion is a big part of this process.

This did not address the whole issue, however. The real problem was that I was still blaming myself for the actions and choices of the abusers. This was a typical co-dependent perception. The responsibility for their conduct was theirs, not mine. After I figured that, it became much easier to deal with my anger because I was on familiar turf, dealing with the very familiar issue of self-blame.

With the first neighbour, I had to make a conscious, educated effort to separate myself from her and leave the responsibility for the one-sided friendship with her. This was the only way to move on and not be constantly angry because I failed to protect myself. I had to separate my feelings of hurt from her actions. It was the same with the other neighbour – his behaviour was because of who he was, not because of anything I had done.

Shifting the responsibility shifted the anger. It was no longer stuck inside of me, because the blame and the burden was no longer with me. They chose to behave the way they did. I was taken advantage of because I was not well. The first person used me even before I started my recovery, and the other managed to use me only once.

In the past I did ignore my senses too many times, but that was because I was not well, mentally and emotionally. This was the compassion I needed. Unlike a narcissist, I was able to reach my authentic self. For decades I was co-dependent but I never completely lost that sense of self. Even in the worst of my depression I knew there was a little candle burning inside me that somehow never went out.

Ignoring my intuition in the past and behaving irrationally was not a reason to beat myself up now. I used acceptance and compassion, and remembered that the only person I could change was myself. After that the anger was no longer inside my chest. I did feel general anger, but it was dispersing rather than burning inside me or making me shake. And this was progress.

Understanding the problem helped me get better. Being a survivor allowed me to look at my reactions honestly and admit that somehow I forgot to use acceptance, compassion and unconditional love, the three most important tools for recovery. Instead I redirected the anger outwards, behaving not unlike a narcissist.

As a survivor I understood that my recovery was about making my everyday life better. That was the good thing about being a survivor – there was a path ahead. I was no longer in the pits of despair and unable to see a way out.

RULES FOR DEALING WITH TOXIC PEOPLE

As I mentioned, meeting toxic people in life is unavoidable. We have to be able to deal with them. To start with, what I found useful was to have two very simple and clear rules for how to behave with predatory people:

SHOW NO EMOTION

Do not react when someone is provoking you. That is when you make mistakes. Always give yourself time to find the best way to deal with the issue.

GIVE NO INFORMATION

Only give very general answers if you have to. In this situation a mobile phone is a very good tool. Say, 'Excuse me, I have to deal with something', then move away while playing with your phone.

To detect toxic people, firstly use your gut reaction, your senses and your past experiences. These, at least, we have plenty of experience with.

CHOOSING NOT TO CARE

Choosing not to care is not about showing others that you don't care. Managing to disconnect emotionally from the toxic person is the best defence there is. In some situations, such as in the work place, you cannot leave so you have to deal with such people in a smarter way. You can be polite and pleasant, and not care at the same time.

The solution to being co-dependent, I found after repeating the same mistakes again and again, is that you don't have to fight the narcissists to defeat them. If you have to be around one, do not give them your emotional energy. Be polite, but unemotional.

As a victim I used to get upset and go on the defence each time my mother attacked my character, and that gave her the upper hand. This is why she used to attack me – because it worked well.

Narcissists are after emotional energy, after your attention and your emotions. Being able to influence you gives them that sense of control and importance. The covert narcissists need that especially. Having social standing and compliant minions keeps their false egos working.

WHAT ABOUT THE GOOD PEOPLE OUT THERE?

Not all the people we meet are narcissists, of course. There are good people out there, but it takes time to find out what someone is like.

One helpful rule I can suggest is to be polite towards everyone new you meet. Being rude is showing weakness, and it is unpleasant and unnecessary. Putting everyone off is a reactive and unhealthy behaviour. For a period of time I found myself doing exactly that and it was not helpful in any way. You might notice I used 'polite', and avoided using the word 'nice', because it has a different connotation when it comes to the children of narcissists. We will come to that later.

As I mentioned before, the whole idea of thriving is to not be affected by toxic people. But at the survivor stage of recovery I was facing another anger problem, and it was a rather big one at that.

ANGER AT THE NARCISSISTIC PARENT AND MY FAMILY OF ORIGIN

As I mentioned at the start, I had managed to successfully have no contact with my family for years, and I had managed to deal with many of my issues. However, I still experienced anger when I thought about my toxic family of origin and about the damage the narcissistic abuse did to me.

Was this the same issue I have already talked about? Was I angry because I let the abuse happen until I was forty years old despite the fact I knew something was very wrong? This is a fair question, and the answer is that this is no doubt partly true. I was angry at myself for remaining a victim for so long, and for betraying my good senses and my authentic feelings. But this anger was so much deeper and harder to deal with. It had roots right back to my early upbringing and the very formation of my identity.

The matter wasn't helped by the memories that kept on surfacing. I will share some of them before going into all the aspects of this important issue. These memories were like little pieces of a puzzle put together by my mind when I was not even trying to remember. They just happened as I was doing some everyday task.

These memories were not flashbacks, because they did not make me flinch with shame. It was painful to remember, but I felt the pain in the area of my chest, and it was not the urgent feeling I currently experienced in my mind as a flashback. I just went 'Wow, I can't believe I forgot about that.' I think my brain was finding the memories that were stuffed right in the back, because I was unable to cope or process them at the time.

Example:

I remembered something quite disturbing about my first experience with depression as a young teenager. During the school holidays I used to go to the movies alone. The weekday daytime screenings had only a few people in the big theatres. On a few occasions, during the screening men would sit next to me with jackets over their crotches. I used to freeze and feel too embarrassed to move. There was so little self-esteem, so little fight left in me, that I could not find the strength to offend them by moving.

Remembering that gave me the chills. Processing this memory with my adult brain made me realise I was the perfect victim for sexual predators – I was the lonely child that would not run to her parents because she was too ashamed that bad things were happening to her. I don't think I could have screamed even if I was attacked on the street – my voice was dull and wedged in my throat. I felt I had so little right to exist I literally could not make a fuss to save my life. In my family I was conditioned to abuse, so there was no surprise I later attracted all sorts of predators.

As a child of a narcissist you have your own stories, I am sure. The abuse took our voice and our identities. In this respect the anger we feel is justified, as the anger of all victims of abuse is justified. At the same time it can be very detrimental to the healing process. More about that later.

Another example:

Other memories were quite trivial, but now I was able put them in a new context because I was familiar with the patterns of narcissistic behaviour.

As someone with no self-esteem my state of mind used to be affected by my circumstances and by the company I found myself in. Moving to a new school and finding three new girlfriends was a good period for me. Their compliments lifted my spirit, and I even started wearing a skirt instead of my usual pair of old jeans. The first time my mother saw me she squinted, lifted her chin and said, 'I like you better in trousers.' That was it.

What she said did not feel very uplifting, but it was the first time she had ever said 'I like you', so I was very confused. She managed to make me doubt that I looked good in a skirt while also making me doubt that she had said anything mean.

Now I know that covert narcissists are masters of such double-edged remarks. And now I know the remark had nothing to do with the skirt, but it had to do with the positive change in me. In this fortunate period during my teenage years, for a moment I felt pretty and confident, and that did not sit well with my mother's narcissistic agenda.

Understanding such memories from the past helped my recovery. And remembering was not necessarily a bad thing – it gave me a chance to process these memories. Remembering what happened to me, however, came with a great deal of anger and negative emotions. This was not so good, and my mind kept going back to the past and re-experiencing negative emotions.

Eventually I identified two different types of anger I was experiencing – a good, helpful anger, and one that was detrimental and hindered my recovery. Before I get to the bad anger I will cover the good anger, because I believe it saved my life.

HOW GOOD ANGER SAVED MY LIFE

Anger is an emotion, and it is there to bring one's attention to something that is a threat or a violation, something that is detrimental to a person. It is a pressing and unpleasant feeling that urges action.

During my early depressive episodes the anger I was feeling was mainly against myself. I used to hit myself on the head because I was so ugly and so stupid. I was internalising the dysfunctionality of the toxic family as my own fault and my failure of character.

During my later episodes the anger had disappeared, and all I felt was something between pain and dread. It was a dull feeling of desperately needing something to run on, something to pick me up. I felt empty and powerless.

My latest depressive episode was the worst; I talked about it in detail in my first book. At the time I was in my late-thirties and I had a complete breakdown. I ended up on the kitchen floor screaming at the top of my lungs. Normal life appeared impossible and I had intense suicidal thoughts. It was the first time I experienced destructive anger directed at the world rather than myself.

This is when my mother found her way back into my life. She nearly managed to push me over the edge by attacking the invisible wounds from my childhood – character, appearance, and being ill. This is when I noticed she was glowing with self-satisfaction – narcissists feel at their best when their supply is down. This is when I finally understood my mother would never show me empathy or concern.

THE LITTLE BIRD STORY

At this time I started pulling away from my mother in a way I never had before. I had refused to go to see her and even started to put the phone down when she offended me. This generated in her a great deal of rage and dismay.

In line with the push-pull games of the narcissists, the moment you pull away they attempt to bring you back under their influence by changing tactics.

This is where the little bird came in. My mother found it in the garden, rescued it, and called me to tell me all about it. She was excited and going on and on about it. Come on, what kind of a monster would not side with her over a little bird?

Devaluation, then distraction – it was a move by a master. There was no more criticism about me taking medication, or comments about my weight and hair, or anything about me. Suddenly the topic was changed. In fact, she was talking about the bird so keenly, I pictured her as a photographer yelling 'Look at the bird! Look at the bird!' to get my attention where she wanted it.

In that very moment, holding the phone in my hand, something clicked inside my brain, a sudden understanding of what was happening. I was in such pain I wanted to die, and my mother was talking about a bird. Normally I would not argue the hierarchy of importance, but this time I did. I was not less important than a bird, and this moment felt like a mental gasp. The ugly mess inside me separated, anger rose as layers of muck fell. Something inside me demanded that I had a value of some sort, I had abilities and even worth, and yet I was on the brink of self-destruction, and it was not fair.

This new-found sense had risen out of desperation. I was missing something important, I could feel it, I could taste it. Something was messing with me, it kept tripping me up and knocking me down. There was something unfair about the fact I ended up in pieces and screaming on the kitchen floor. And for the first time I was angry about that. Really angry.

I guess many victims have found their voice in the depths of despair. Narcissistic abuse increases with time, especially with those who try to pull away from the narcissist and self-preservation in the victims finally kicks in.

Anger, I found, could be a driving force, and it was much better than depression. In my case I simply put down the phone. I knew I had to get away from my mother permanently if I was to survive.

Now, as a survivor, I understand that the narcissist's power is in the illusion and in their ability to destroy the identity of their victims in order to control them. I managed to recover and feel as valuable as any human being. Since then, the desperation I used to feel has become just a memory.

I had processed many memories like this one, but I still felt profound anger about the abuse I went through in my family of origin. I know I felt this anger for a reason, and I know it saved me.

The last episode of depression I mentioned was the very first time I felt anger against the world and the fact I was in such pain and no one seemed to care or understand. It made me search for answers. Not long after, I came across information about childhood emotional abuse and parents with personality disorders, and I began my recovery.

GOOD ANGER

Honouring my anger was about me. Anger was important to me in my first stages of getting better. I guess it was still important. It was there to keep me safe. I played the narcissistic game, even in my adulthood, because I was conditioned to do so, and my anger was there to stop this from happening again. It was a driving force, because it helped me do the things I would otherwise avoid, as my co-dependent habits dictated.

I understood that the abuse was destructive at such a fundamental level that it was likely to be in my mind for a very long time. I did, however, expect the anger to subside with time, as the healing process progressed. Facing and experiencing the anger in an authentic way was supposed to dissipate it.

In my case it continued to reoccur on a daily basis and I figured I had to find a different way to approach the issue.

DEALING WITH THE GOOD ANGER

Anger is an emotion driven mostly by fear and uncertainty. I had to face the issues that were worrying me.

One source of anxiety was the possibility of my toxic family coming after me and how I would react to their presence face to face.

Another fear was that my mother could get to the people in my life, or to those of them she still had an access to, and turn them against me. I kept imagining situations in which she had managed to do just that, and my reactions to them.

Wondering about such things was not surprising; after a prolonged torment the brain tries to protect against any future eventualities of experiencing the same pain.

I found the answer to both concerns was to simply prepare for such events as best as I could. Having a plan was supposed to greatly ease the anxiety. So I tried to do exactly that.

Would my mother manipulate the people in my life against me if she could? Yes, of course. It had happened throughout my life and it was likely to happen again. Given the chance, my mother would do the most damage that she could.

What could I do about it? Nothing. I had to simply let go.

The simple truth was that what others chose to believe was out of my control. What I could do was be authentic and let others be what they would be. And, most importantly, I had to be prepared to carry on despite anyone close to me falling under the spell of the narcissist.

This was getting my power back for good – being able to stand completely alone and know who I was. Only then I could be free of my narcissistic mother.

This was the right answer, as a survivor I knew that. Clearly any fear I had with this issue was connected to my own insecurities. Getting over such fears was accepting what could happen and knowing I could carry on despite the fallout from the narcissistic slander. There is so much freedom in letting go of the opinions of others, and I believe most survivors know that already.

But what about the anger that came from expecting a future encounter with my abusive family of origin?

The question was, how would I react to a face-to-face encounter after all this time? The tendency to freeze and get defensive was very much what my co-dependent behaviour used to be about. Would I be able to handle myself now?

I found what worked to calm my anxiety was to prepare for a potential encounter of the abusive kind, and to have a clear plan of action in my head. This was about my wellbeing, and not about them.

I put some very simple rules on paper and learned them by heart. I had to do this in order to reduce the element of surprise. The point of making those easy rules was to memorise them well, then simply follow the plan.

RULES FOR UNEXPECTED ENCOUNTERS DURING NO CONTACT

No emotions. No explanations. Use simple sentences and repeat them in a level, polite voice. Indifference is the key word, and a polite and levelled voice achieves just that.

'I will not tolerate any more abuse. I don't want you in my life. Leave now, please.'

If they ask why, the only thing to do is assert yourself with: 'You will respect my decision and you will leave now.'

If they keep on talking at you, no matter what they say, just repeat like a broken record: 'I don't want to talk to you. I don't want to see you. Stay out of my life.' Or whatever phrases you choose.

Do not answer questions. Do not explain your choices. Do not argue. Do not play the blame game. Be polite. Be firm.

...

My plan was pretty simple. It was about not leaving any cracks for anyone to get into my head with words and pull me into another cycle of abuse.

If your narcissistic parent has other children to focus on, you are not in so much danger. But if you are the only available supply, it is possible they might come after you. Needless to say, do not let any abusers into your home. Just say, politely, 'You are not welcome in my house.' Being polite is very important. For someone wanting to see your emotions, being polite is like a bucket of cold water.

If you are in someone else's house, it is likely a setup. Just say politely and nicely that you no longer put up with abusive people, then leave. Do not engage in any other conversation. If they try to stop you, say 'Please stop harassing me.' Remember the polite voice. Or if you feel calm and confident enough, just look at them, pause, smile nicely and simply say 'No'.

The problem with childhood narcissistic abuse is that it quite badly damages our ability to stand up for ourselves. If, however, there is a plan, you can just stick with it, word for word, and avoid confusion. If the narcissist is desperate, it is likely they might try the crocodile tears and try to make you feel bad and look bad in front of others. You should not let this affect you, because you are only responsible for yourself.

Remember: No emotions. Be polite. Be firm. Leave.

...

Thriving, of course, means not having to even think about how we are going to behave, because the outcome of such meetings would be irrelevant to our wellbeing. But if you are not there yet, take this small step. Being prepared reduces the fear and the anger. It reduced mine significantly, so I could carry on with my recovery.

This is why it is important to have the legal stuff sorted around no contact, to make sure your abusers don't obtain the legal power parents get in cases of accidents and emergencies. I knew if something unfortunate happened to me I would be in danger again, and this is why my anger was there – to make me take action and prevent this from happening.

In my case it was obvious that my toxic parents were keeping an eye on me from a distance. They tried to contact my husband twice, and used his work-related site to try to find out more about our plans. Somehow they knew where we were physically, and this was disturbing because only a few people knew that we had moved.

All attempts to get information were from a distance, of course. Covert narcissists are also called vulnerable narcissists, because they are afraid of getting narcissistic injuries. If they are not in a position to abuse, it is likely they will stay away. From a distance, however, they can still interfere with our lives.

My mother was blocked from my email for years, but that did not stop her from giving my address to someone she met on the street, a girlfriend who had scammed me for money in the past. Seeing that name again in my mailbox was a bad surprise, but I knew what to do about it – absolutely nothing.

Remember: Do not react. Do not make contact. Do not answer the email. Do not get involved.

This was exactly what I did. I never heard from this person again.

So, as long as I was independent and strong, it was unlikely my dysfunctional family would come after me. Things could go back to the way they were only if I was broken again. I knew that if I was unable to look after and protect myself, my mother would make her way into my life faster than you can say 'narcissistic abuse'.

This is the relationship toxic parents are after – being in a position to abuse. Otherwise they don't get to feel superior or to discharge their negativity. Keep in mind, when left behind the covert narcissists can become very vindictive, and being prepared pays off.

If you are on the same page as me about no contact, I would suggest that you prepare for any eventuality. For example, If you become mentally incapacitated in an accident make sure your parents cannot make decisions on your behalf. There are legal ways to take away their parental right to make medical decisions and take control over your estate. (This has to be done according to the laws of your country of residence, of course.)

Doing this gave me more confidence that I was out of reach for good.

I fully expect I will be disowned, and I have no issue with that. Of course this is a very personal decision. Depending on the degree of toxicity of your parents, some of you may have chosen to keep a legal contact. Family money is important to those who have to care for children, and to those who are too sick to cope with life. In these cases this advice is not useful at all, but there may be other relevant resources available. Keep on looking, someone will have managed to thrive in this situation, and follow their advice if it feels right for you.

THE BAD ANGER

So far the good anger was about me and my recovery. Good anger worked to my advantage. The bad anger did not. The bad anger was about the narcissist and the other toxic people from the past, but it was directed at them in the present. It was about engaging my thoughts with people who were nowhere near me in the present.

That is the anger that took my time, it took resources, and it affected my mood without having any benefits for me. It drained the joy out of me.

The bad anger was about concerning myself with my toxic family of origin outside of the context of processing memories, ensuring safety, and healing.

On the positive side, I was fully aware this was a remnant of my disorder, and I was trying to resolve it.

This inability to let go of people who were no longer in my life was a result of enmeshment and trauma bond. I experienced bad anger because my borders were not yet as strong as they needed to be.

ENMESHMENT AND BAD ANGER

As a survivor I knew plenty about enmeshment. I will summarise this briefly before I get to what I didn't know about it.

Enmeshment means experiencing the feelings of other family members as your own.

For me, for example, it was taking on the feelings of my narcissistic mother – when she felt bad I felt bad, when she was worried about money I was worried about money, when she was complaining about my brother or father, I became upset. When she was happy, I was relieved. Enmeshment was the need to feel what emotional state my mother was in, in order to behave accordingly.

This, of course, is one of the signs of a dysfunctional family – the children are not allowed to be happier than the parents. The children are expected to look after the emotional state of the parents, no matter how unrealistic this expectation is.

In families with narcissistic mothers enmeshment is unavoidable. The mother is unable to separate her feelings from those of her children and acknowledge them as separate persons. The goal is not to raise independent people, but to provide a convenient and compliant supply.

When my narcissistic mother was angry and upset, she made sure I was as well. It was her way of discharging her negative feelings. As a result of that everyday assault on my mind I felt her feelings in my heart. It was automatic. My mother didn't want to know about mine, of course. Narcissists have a one-sided relationship with the world.

My father's coping strategy was to find faults with the world and that included his children. Much like my narcissistic mother, he passed his shame and negativity down to his children. This is what made him toxic.

In my family I was told my parents did everything for me, so when they were angry about something not going their way, they were angry at me as well. It seemed normal when I was a child, because it was all I knew. As a result my mother could control me just with looks of disgust, and my father with his customary disappointment. I instantly felt their feelings as mine.

In dysfunctional families the parents do not explain themselves, they have the authority to devalue and to demand loyalty. They cannot be questioned, they do not make mistakes, and they do not apologise. Over time the borders of the children are so distorted by the demands of the parents that there is hardly a person left inside.

You probably recognise elements from such enmeshment in your families of origin. Feeling the feelings of others is acknowledging their values and experiences, but not getting the same back is devaluing yours. The young brains adapt to the abusive environment and reprogramming becomes difficult. The slow process of degradation is mixed with the ideas of family and love, and the victims grows up with self-blame and confusion.

...

So far, this was enmeshment as I understood it.

As a survivor I had to face the fact that I have been separated from my family of origin for years, and the anger I felt now came from inside of me. I had to look for the solution there, because the damage was there. My family of origin was still embedded in my head, because enmeshment was the norm for decades. They were in my head even when they were physically far away.

Having that feeling of being enmeshed was as persistent as having the feeling of being anxious and unhappy, or the need to hide who I was and what I felt. It was a default setting in my brain, and I was struggling to change those established neural connections.

ENMESHMENT AND ANGER

I knew what enmeshment was, I had read widely about it, yet for some time I did not realise the connection between my anger and the enmeshment. I was angry because I was struggling to separate myself. My family of origin was a part of my psyche, and admitting that was the first step to doing just that.

My anger was driven by fear as well as frustration and the need for change. Did you feel my anger in my description of enmeshment? I had this desire to throw the bad things back to where they came from, yet they kept on coming back to me. By wanting to give back the abuse in order to feel better, I engaged in enmeshment myself. I was putting a condition on my happiness, and it was that my abusers paid the price for their actions. In reality, they were not in my life and my recovery was entirely up to me.

So, clearly, a great deal of my energy was still going towards my toxic family of origin when, in fact, they were currently nowhere near me. And this was the bad anger I felt.

Before looking at the solutions for this anger, let's have a quick look at trauma bond.

BAD ANGER AND TRAUMA BOND

Another notorious issue to deal with is the childhood bond we have with our parents. Trauma bond is a physiological term that applies in this case. It involves the receiving of some good treatment from the abusers, and becoming addicted to seeking that in the relationship.

Children crave the positive regard of their parents, it ensures safety and belonging. This is why the trauma bond is so strong. As a little child you invest so much effort in the relationship.

Trauma bonding has to do with the random reinforcement of reward and punishment, and with trying to get a good outcome again and again. These good moments in the relationship create a chemical bond. This creates a preoccupation with the abuser and their state of mind, and with trying to predict their actions to achieve the desired result.

The uncertainty of the outcome is why we pay such close attention to the narcissistic parent, and this is really what they want from us. The hurt and pain become a part of our connection to the abuser.

You probably experienced this dynamic as a child – forever trying to please the narcissistic parent, but never succeeding in the long term. Covert narcissists break down their children in stages, by giving them some approval and validation then taking it away. My narcissistic mother could be quite pleasant when things were going well for her. Needless to say, she was good for just long enough to confuse me, then continued to devalue and belittle me.

When I broke down visibly in the past, for example, the abuse stopped for a while, because the goal of the abuse was to keep me down and not to break me altogether. The family needed a scapegoat not a burden.

Unfortunately I did not understand this for a long time, and the confusion I felt was the key. My brain created all kinds of anxiety chemicals, but I did not know what to focus on and what to do to protect me.

BORDERS AND THE BAD ANGER

Enmeshment, trauma bond, and any abuse are pretty much about deforming or destroying the borders that protect the victim, physically or emotionally. They are about reducing the victim so the abuser can have the upper hand in all circumstances.

The bad anger I was experiencing had a lot to do with that. My borders were not yet strong enough to keep me safe, and the danger of another narcissistic assault was still there.

Borders are essential, as essential as self-care. Without borders every encounter can be emotionally abrasive, because the outcome is perceived as being directly attached to the value of the person without borders. In the past, if someone said a half-hearted hello to me, I thought it was because of what they thought of me, not because they had something else on their mind, for example.

As a survivor I had learned my value was not attached to the reactions of others. So in similar situations the feeling was there, but I was able to process it and dismiss it quickly. It was progress. It was a slow progress, however, because it involved a great deal of purposeful processing. Maintaining my borders took much hard work.

All mental health professionals talk about the importance of borders, and they all agree the way to keep your borders strong is to develop a healthy ego, because trying to combat each bad thing, one by one, is difficult and time consuming. There is no way you can individually process every encounter during the day and follow complicated rules about protecting yourself.

The goal of recovery is to develop a healthy ego inside, then the borders become automatic.

I had to focus my attention on that rather than on the abusive people in the present. I had to go back to basics, and use acceptance, compassion and unconditional love. Later in the book I will talk about other tools of recovery, and more about developing a healthy ego and strong sense of identity.

For me, just understanding where the bad anger was coming from was a good start, but it was not enough. I needed to look for practical solutions.

SOLUTIONS FOR GETTING RID OF THE BAD ANGER

As I have said, bad anger was about the narcissist, and I had wasted so much time on them already. I found wishing they would just disappear from the face of the Earth was not helpful. It was the anger of a victim, and I decided I was no longer that.

While looking for answers I came across an explanation that instantly resonated with me. It was as follows: Thinking about the narcissist who is no longer around is like opening your borders to reach out all the way to them. Every time you do that you open a big hole in your borders, and the narcissist comes right back through this hole, and back into your head.

While visualising that, I had a physical reaction. I went 'Yuck!' because this was definitely not what I wanted. It was true, though. The narcissist was far away, and it was me who was initiating the opening of the borders and letting her back in.

After that, each time I caught my thoughts reaching out I visualised the narcissist coming back like a boomerang, and this was so distressing I managed to interrupt my thought process and take charge.

Thinking back, this was very similar to the way I stopped my inner critic. And looking way back, it was the same reason I went looking for medical help when I needed surgery, despite my mother's gaslighting. And, finally, it was the same reason I chose no contact – it was the sense of self-preservation. Realising how much damage certain things did to me activated a very primal brain function.

The sense of self-preservation can be strong even when one's brain is dysregulated, because it is a domain of the older part of the brain, much like fear, hunger and bodily reflexes.

As the abuse from my mother escalated, for example, my biological instinct for self-preservation kicked in. It felt like I was on the edge of a cliff and my mother was ready to push me over at any moment.

I sensed a clear danger, and this shifted my focus from the devastating self-loathing I was experiencing at the time.

A healthy brain responds properly to threats and damage, which is pretty much what self-care is about. This is a new frontier for children of narcissists, however, because we are used to small amounts of damage having been inflicted regularly on us ever since we were born.

This is why people struggle to understand narcissistic abuse. For most, self-preservation and self-care are integral parts of existence. Why would someone put up with abuse, or self-harm instead of walking away? It seems like a very unreasonable thing to do.

The answer is, of course, that the egos of such people are very damaged. This was inflicted upon them, but most people cannot comprehend that. The good news is that we, adult children of narcissists, can get better, and this is exactly what this book is about.

So, visualising helped me see that thinking about the narcissist who was far away was harming me. The anger was the emotion that was trying to alert me to it.

Unfortunately, without connecting with the frontal lobe, and without a clear understanding of what is happening, the older part of the brain can create a very bad situation, where the angrier we are the more we think about the things we are angry about.

This is why this visualising was helpful – I was able to see clearly that I was doing something that was hurting me.

On the positive side, at this stage I was starting to become quite comfortable inside my borders. It was becoming a good space for me, because I was treating myself well most of the time. I only had troubles with other people still invading my space, and I had to work more on that.

Another similar technique for combating bad anger was to use reason and logic. This was about catching the intrusive thoughts, challenging the point of such thoughts, and changing them into something more sensible and useful.

For example, 'I hate these people because they did this and this to me,' can be changed to 'I want these people out of my life.' The first statement is getting caught up in a trap of negativity, and the second is exactly what is needed – getting rid of the toxic people. You know which one makes sense.

The technique is about interrupting the damaging pattern by asking the sensible questions, 'What is the use of this? What do I get out of it?' It is about putting more effort into what we want. This way we are much more likely to achieve what we want.

So, again, these techniques were about realising clearly that something was damaging to me, and then even my dysregulated brain agreed there had to be a better way.

These techniques were helpful, but there was something else that finally made a big difference.

But before I try to explain the breakthrough that drastically improved my mental state, I have to explain why some bad experiences result in a long-lasting trauma, while some bad experiences do not.

Please bear with me for just a little longer.

WHAT CONSTITUTES TRAUMA

As I was going about my everyday business another memory surfaced, and it was not what you would expect.

During my second major depressive episode I remembered an unusually rebellious period of time. After taking a year off university I was in a bad way. I kept drinking alcohol just to keep functioning. I had a job in a shabby bar, stayed out all night and dated the most unsuitable men. It felt like if I was to stop and think about what I was doing, I was going to lose my mind. Eventually I became exhausted and very sick. This was at a time when I was trying to cure my severe depression by acting out like never before and hoping that changing my behaviour would change my state of mind.

I clearly remembered this dark period of my life, but I was surprised at how very distant the memories felt. The question was, of course, why? Why had these memories faded in my middle-aged brain, while at the same time some silly childhood story could bring me to a flood of tears? At the time this period was very distressing to me. For a long time afterwards I felt deeply disturbed by my behaviour.

The only thing I could think of was that I had processed the memories somehow. The way I behaved was clearly very damaging, and I should have never gone there. I felt very guilty at the time. There was no ambiguity about it, hard lessons were learned, and the memories had faded.

So, how did this compare to the years of covert abuse, and my brain struggling to understand what was happening?

Clearly a lesson learned was a processed memory. Trauma was about failing to see a solution, and failing to take any sensible actions to get better. This seemed to be a likely answer, because a result of growing up in dysfunction is not being able to tell what is up and what is down. I simply could not tell what was happening, and I could not see a way out.

The entrapment and the failure to see a solution drove my self-destructive behaviour, and it was the reason behind the many depressive episodes I went through. I was struggling to make sense of the degradation I experienced growing up, and I was a participating player in the abuse for many years.

The early childhood trauma was imprinted on my brain because I was a very well-behaved child, trying very hard to be liked, yet I was disliked and humiliated because of who I was. There was no solution to that. This was the genuine solidified trauma left in my head, and this was why I could still feel the bitter taste in my mouth, and feel the lump in my throat, and why I had the urge to cry each time I re-experienced the emotional abuse.

Children of narcissists are stuck with the personality disorder of their parents. The brain cannot cope easily with conflicting messages, especially when the blame is placed solely on the victim. Being called bad when I was so good that I was a doormat – this was what created the lasting childhood trauma I was still dealing with.

This is what I understood before the breakthrough I mentioned earlier. So let us go back to the bad anger, and how to deal with it.

BAD ANGER AND MY FINAL BREAKTHROUGH

I will try to describe what happened in my case, and what helped me deal with my anger and move on.

During one long road trip in my car my mind kept on going back to the past and 'how could they do this to me?' and I felt very, very fed up with this pointless reoccurring thought. I was a forty-five-year-old woman, and I had to find a way to cross this mind swamp and move on.

I already knew that the brain needed to understand and learn in order to store the memories in the past. This was quite straightforward – processing meant understanding what happened and what could be done in the future in order to avoid the same danger and pain.

So I started thinking about trauma, and what could possibly be the lesson I had failed to learn. What was my brain still trying to figure out?

It was a good question. Obviously there was something else I had to learn in order to heal from my toxic family of origin. I had to work out why I was going back to 'how could they do this to me?' again and again. I already knew the answers to why they treated me the way they did. I knew why, and I knew how; there was hardly a question unanswered about that.

But what was the lesson I had failed to learn?

It felt like there was a knot in my brain, something unclear I was getting caught up in, and I was going around in circles rather than leaning towards the pain, getting through it, and reaching the other side.

And then it came to me, a very straightforward thought. It surfaced like an epiphany. That full array of negativity towards me, from pettiness to disappointment, and from disgust to hatred, those were my parents' real feelings about me. They were not pretending, or play-acting, or doing something to confuse me. Those were simply their genuine feelings about me. It was my childhood denial that stopped me accepting that very simple and very straightforward truth.

There was a wall of denial preventing me from seeing that. I had been hitting this wall for a long time, and finally it crumbled.

I felt a clear direct connection between my parents and me, and I felt the full impact of their negativity and hatred coming straight at me. This was not the fluffy, tangled, intellectual realization that 'I was not loved'. No. I was disliked, even as a child. And I was hated as an adult. And somehow I only understood this clearly at that very moment.

I felt a hot wave from my head to my toes, and that was it. I accepted I was hated, and this was perfectly fine. I just felt the anger drain and turn into a mild bemusement. I was nothing like my parents, no wonder they hated me.

It was amazing and slightly bamboozling that something so simple and straightforward worked so well. The knot in my brain disappeared and I managed to separate myself from the past and from my family of origin.

WHAT HAPPENED, REALLY?

I will try to explain this experience better.

As a small child I refused to accept that my parents had such negative feelings towards me. It felt like a burning in the stomach, and I winced and twitched, and convinced myself that these were not really their feelings. It was too much, or it was too scary. Something in me said 'no, I do not want to go there', and a block was created. It was the childhood denial, the knot, the barrier I kept on hitting that was preventing me from moving forwards emotionally. It was the manipulations, and the enmeshment, and the trauma bond all rolled together.

And it was so simple. When the barrier disappeared and I experienced the feeling of being hated, it was fine. At forty-five, accepting my parents hated me was easy. So easy, it was a little funny. I felt myself being repelled from my family of origin rather than being drawn towards them.

This took away all that anger I was feeling and could not understand. The danger was clear, and the action I needed to take was clear.

Strange, I know. Years of trying, then it just happened. A professional therapist may have got me there much faster, but somehow I managed to finally make the breakthrough.

WHAT ELSE I UNDERSTOOD

I understood that the feelings of my dysfunctional parents belonged to them and should stay with them. I was a separate human being, and my feelings were what mattered. I continued on with my new-found unconditional self-love, and was firmly on the way to recovery.

As an adult I understood that parents hating their children was not something strange or unlikely. It happened everywhere, and much of the trauma people carried came from their family of origin and early childhood.

Accepting I was hated set me free, because I could finally be firmly on my own side. The power of narcissistic parents is in the heads of their children. That is why my anger was so persistent; it was trying to make it through this incredible denial, through this thick knot in my subconscious.

Ultimately, the solution was entirely with me. And it was very much worth making the journey to finally find the way to separate myself from my family of origin.

WHERE TO LOOK FOR SOLUTIONS

So far, you may have noticed, all the solutions I found had to do with changing myself, because this was where the problems were – in my head. The damage was there.

As survivors we know plenty about narcissistic wounds and why we react the way we do. When the narcissist calls us bad, for example, we react because we feel the hurt inside of us. The narcissistic parent may have made the wounds initially, but now it is up to us to heal them.

On the positive side, this is what we have the power to do – change ourselves. And as we start to feel better, it gets easier to do so.

I noticed that in my first book I put a great deal of effort into defending myself and proving the damage the narcissistic upbringing did to me. Even as a survivor I caught myself doing that.

From now on I will try to focus on my recovery and what I had to change about myself, my thinking and my behaviour. For example, I had to admit that, inside, I still cared if others thought I was a bad person. I had to be seen to be good, and that was something coming from my childhood.

Do try something with me. Decide you are a bad person for a while. Let's be annoying, and argumentative, and demanding. So what? As if the world around us is good? It isn't. We have the right to fit in and to behave badly if we have to.

For me, deciding who I was, even if that happened to be a bad person, put me in charge in my own head. In charge of who I was. Good or bad, it was me. And I liked myself, good or bad.

MORE ABOUT RECOVERY

For a long time I was doing great, then something embarrassing would happen and I would become upset with myself and wonder how long it would take for me to recover. Finally it became clear to me that recovery was not about never again having awkward moments, but about carrying merrily on my way despite them popping up left and right each day.

It was not about me becoming some new, easy-going, smooth person, but about coping well despite the everyday ups and downs. The hard moments in life never just disappear. I simply started reacting differently to the daily challenges and moving on with my best interests at heart.

ABOUT MEMORY PROCESSING

We do have a great power to understand and change our behaviour with reason and logic. Before I get to the C-PTSD and the things that are not easy to change that way, there are a few points worth mentioning about our abilities to deal with traumatic experiences.

I came across some research on natural disasters and trauma, specifically on earthquakes. Earthquakes may leave lasting trauma years after the event. The researchers found that people who were in a position to do something physically, such as to run away when the quake happened, had significantly fewer issues with trauma than those who were inside buildings and could do nothing but wait. Going into a flight mode helped release some of the energy produced by the body as a reaction to the sudden life-threatening event.

Not surprisingly, it has been established that feelings of defeat and entrapment lead to a much greater suicide risk. Helplessness and defeat are the results of being unable to escape a situation, like small children who cannot escape the family they are born in.

This is why it is important to process traumatic experiences in order to overcome the state of learned helplessness.

Normal people remember bad memories, but the emotions attached have faded. This makes sense – a lesson is learned without paying the emotional price each time you remember. This is a smart way to learn, and a healthy brain can do exactly that.

The brain of a survivor of narcissistic abuse is dysregulated, and it recalls some memories as if they are happening in the present. The emotions are strong, the body's reactions are still physical and the experience is still overwhelming each time the memory comes to mind.

I had many bad memories stored appropriately in the past. But I still had some bad memories that were reoccurring in the 'now'. Emotions were stored unprocessed, in a child-like state. Those were often memories connected with toxic shame. My brain was unable to process such memories, because shame does not provide solutions or a way out of bad situations. Toxic shame is just a heavy feeling which weighs you down.

When such memories begin to build, the brain cannot function well. The constant state of low anxiety shifts the brain into survival mode, and a wide range of brain functions are no longer performed.

As a survivor I had dealt with the emotional flashbacks quite successfully by going through a quick process of recognising what they were and reminding myself I was safe. I had become quite good at it. So I did something similar with processing the memories – by going through the fog and to the other side, where the memory was understood and resolved emotionally.

To process the emotions in these memories, I had to take the child away from the memory and make her see how unhealthy the toxic shame was through the eyes of an adult. And, as an adult, I had to create the new pathways in the brain to override the sense of inner worthlessness associated with such memories.

The young version of me now understood what was happening and why, because the adult version of me could understand it, of course. The story became different.

As you probably know it takes long time to deal with the memories one by one, but one gets better and better with practice. And, most of all, the brain learns that this is a good thing.

If you are currently tired of going over and over stuff like that, and you still feel the pain weighing you down, well, here are some words of encouragement – I felt like that for a long time, but eventually it got easier.

If, however, you feel worse, it is time to get professional help. Personally, I only felt better, or I felt the same for some time, but I was not getting worse.

This is a self-help book, and it is based on my personal experience. I hope if you are reading this you have made the transition from a victim to a survivor, and you are on the path to recovery.

So far, as survivors, we have managed to push back the bulk of the issues that were crushing us, so we can breathe again. 'Thriving' is about getting all of this out of the way and standing up strong.

PART II: Emotional Dysregulation and Complex PTSD

So far, you may have noticed, my attempts to deal with anger used reason and logic. This means I was using the frontal lobe, the most sophisticated part of the brain. By becoming consciously aware of the trauma, I learned to cope with it.

However, the brain is a complex organ, and it may not respond well to reason when the amygdala is involved. As a survivor you have not only heard of it, but you have also experienced Complex PTSD.

I will quickly summarise what I have learned about the biological side of it. You can research it for yourself; there is plenty of information out there.

THE TRIUNE BRAIN MODEL

According to this model, humans have three functional layers of the brain, which developed throughout evolution:

Reptilian brain – This is the oldest part of the brain, responsible for survival and for the regulation of the breathing, body temperature, heartbeat, and basic metabolic functions linked to survival. It responds to images rather than language, and does not learn well. It is associated with survival and safety.

Limbic system – This is the emotional brain (Mammalian brain), associated with remembering strong emotions, looking for pleasure and avoiding pain. It is responsible for motivation, learning and memory.

Neocortex – This is the newest part of the brain, responsible for reason and logic, consciousness and abstract thoughts, and for making decisions. It can become overpowered by the emotional brain when it comes to primary tasks.

Talking about the brain, we definitely have to mention the amygdalae, which are part of the limbic system. We have two of these, and they are referred to as the amygdala part of the brain, responsible for remembering emotions like fear and anxiety, and for the physiological responses of fight and flight.

The mechanical responses of the amygdalae are linked to C-PTSD, because trauma situations are interpreted as life-threatening situations. Prolonged stress and constant activation of the endocrine system lead to adrenal fatigue. The tightening of the muscles and the irregular breathing patterns are registered in the brain as danger, even when the threat is not physical. It could be a threat is to the ego, or the mental wellbeing of a person, but it is registered as physical danger by the amygdala.

So far so good. It makes sense, I thought, as I was reading about this evolution of the brain and the reasons it favours survival before happiness. So far my frontal lobe had done a great job of clearing the self-hatred, self-blame, toxic shame and people-pleasing, but anxiety and fear continued to be a problem.

When the amygdalae are involved it is hard to reason with fear, especially when it is from an early childhood trauma. So, although I had gained a very good understanding of narcissism and what happened during my childhood and beyond, sometimes my body kept reacting the same way it did when I was a small dependent child.

WHAT IS COMPLEX-PTSD

Experiencing C-PTSD is the feeling of being easily overwhelmed, easily angered, or the opposite – disassociating instead of taking action when needed. Most survivors of childhood abuse know that dealing with C-PTSD is hard, because the adrenal and nervous systems have been out of balance for many years. Chronic trauma changes the body and the brain. Dysfunctional families create dysfunctional people. That is us, survivors of childhood abuse, and we need to face this dysfunction.

One of the tell-tale symptoms of C-PTSD is brain fog. I am sure you are familiar with the experience. I was, I just did not have a name for it. And 'brain fog' is a very accurate description.

This is my explanation of what that is:

The frontal lobe is a wonder of evolution. It has the ability to absorb so much information and all kinds of input. Humans live in groups, and the children stay in the family and learn for many years, because this is an evolutionary advantage. And we humans came to evolve rather quickly.

Narcissistic parents teach their kids a value system that is detrimental to their wellbeing, like toxic shame and ignoring their needs in order to please others. The learned behaviour is at odds with the older part of the brain, which is responsible for self-preservation in a biological sense. This part wants to keep us safe, but does not know how. The signals it sends are ignored.

In other words, there is a big discrepancy between what we are told, and what we experience. In the case of narcissistic mothers the abuse is mixed with the idea of love and family, and the victims are trapped for years in confusion and repeated trauma.

The way I was taught to behave, for example, was hurting me constantly, and I felt the physical symptoms of stress. Part of my brain was screaming out, metaphorically speaking, and I had physical symptoms because of it, but I continued to behave the way I was conditioned to in my family of origin. I had no idea what would make me feel better.

As a result of this constant conflict both the frontal cortex and the limbic system were not working properly.

Sensitive and receptive children are more likely to respond to emotional abuse with a brain fog because the frontal lobe keeps the 'lower brain' in check. If the frontal lobe fails to do so, the result can be lashing out in anger and confusion. This is why some children become rebellious and out of control as a response to emotional abuse.

A brain fog feels exactly like being in a fog. The brain is simply not working properly, and you find yourself saying and doing unexpected things. You are disconnected from your feelings and needs, and do not even know what is good for you and what is not. This is a dysregulated brain.

Example:

This is an very trivial example of co-dependent unhealthy behaviour – feeling obliged to buy something because the shop assistant has started talking to you and you believe you have to justify the effort she has made.

I talked about this in the first book; it used to happen to me often. It was a very co-dependent experience, as if the shop assistant was inside my head, and she or he mattered so much I could not disappoint them. After that I wondered why I wasted my little money on things I did not want.

This was a ridiculous co-dependent behaviour, and a very persistent one. I kept getting the same impulses way into my recovery, but I no longer acted the way I used to.

When we behave in this old way we are acting against our interests, and putting a random person's interests ahead of our own. Then what about the big things? How can we make decisions about life, about work, about what we want?

We can't. We crash and burn. I know I did.

This is why knowledge is so important. My frontal lobe had to learn how to behave in a new way, as well as to learn to perceive life from a new angle. When that goes on for a long time one's ability to learn and think changes. A brain in survival mode has different priorities.

On the positive side, emotional abuse has much to do with the frontal lobe, and this is the part that is most able and likely to change with recovery. This is why reason and logic work first, and then we have to let the 'lower' brain catch up.

FEAR AND C-PTSD

Many of the C-PTSD symptoms are fear based. Fear is a major part of C-PTSD, because the abuse happens when the caregiver is big and scary, and the child is most vulnerable and susceptible to suggestions.

The fear may be about physical violation or psychological humiliation, both registered as a threat by the amygdalae. Early abuse results in a reduced size of the hippocampus and in overactive amygdalae. As mentioned before, the brain has problems regulating emotions.

This is why C-PTSD can be triggered by small everyday things.

Examples:

When my husband and I bought a house I thought that was it, nothing could disturb me there because I was safe in my own home. I was wrong. The C-PTSD was in me, and it had little to do with where I was.

Every time I heard the front door open when I was not expecting it to open, my heart jumped, then ended down in my stomach, just like when I was a child. It was amazing how persistent that particular reaction was. Many years later, it was still there when I was surprised by the sound of the front door.

Of course, after two seconds I knew what was happening, and I came down quickly. I was not badly affected by this repeated little scare, but it was there. It was like a glitch in my brain, an automatic reaction.

Another C-PTSD reaction I noticed was when I caught somebody watching me in a disapproving manner. Then I would freeze and disassociate in the same way I did when my mother was looking at me. The abuse I received as a child was not physical, but it affected my body physically. The negativity, the frustrated looks, the sounds of disapproval, the tone, the humiliation and minimization, all of these were registered as attacks on me and I had a physical reaction as a response.

I think another C-PTSD reaction was putting up with discomfort. You probably know what I am talking about. For example, sitting in an uncomfortable position, but not doing anything about it even when you can do it easily. The state of discomfort feels somehow so normal that it does not register. I know I had such experiences. It was similar to holding my breath. It was the habit of subconsciously trying not to attract attention to myself.

All this was an echo from my childhood. Being in the same room with my parents evoked tension in my stomach and a sense of awkwardness. It came with their relentless unspoken disapproval. This fear was still with me in my own house. My lizard brain was looking out for danger, and it came with the sudden sound of an opening door.

Another example of emotional dysregulation:

I was moving some furniture and I noticed that a lamp nearby might break as a result, but I carried on. The lamp broke. I cried, not because I cared for the lamp, but because I was so stupid.

My emotional reaction was out of control, it filled my whole head. It took over and I lost any sense of perspective. I kept assuring myself that nothing bad had happened. I was well, and things were well, why on earth would this be such a catastrophe?

It wasn't, of course, it just felt like it was. The overreaction came with a long history of being shamed for breaking things, as a behavioural control.

Apparently I broke a Christmas bauble as a child. I could not recall this event but I was reminded about it each Christmas. The mentioning of the bauble had become a tradition.

Another example I can remember was breaking my bicycle. This provoked an angry outburst by my mother about me breaking things. She demanded I fix the bicycle. I couldn't fix it, the whole frame was mangled out of shape; I fell off at high speed on a concrete road. But, as we know, toxic parents are not reasonable. They use their children's failings as a weapon against them.

As a survivor I did my best to process the broken lamp experience using my frontal lobe. I clearly understood this was an overreaction and I realised that the reason I was so upset was my C-PTSD. Eventually I calmed down and my perspective changed.

Emotional dysregulation is just that – overreacting to triggers from the past. Or underreacting, of course. Unfortunately those triggers can simply be normal parts of life.

Another example:

My local health clinic had mixed my health records with someone else's. This was obviously more serious, but nothing to worry about because I had been a patient there for many years.

What I experienced was more of a dread, and the very familiar 'why is this happening to me?' as if something or someone was targeting me for reasons unknown. The failure of the clinic had something to do with me and my ineptitude in life.

Does that sound familiar? Adult children of narcissists know this reaction. It comes with a long history of taking the blame when problems occur.

I dealt with such experiences with the help of reason and logic. The reasons for the anxiety in the first place, however, had little to do with reason or logic.

THE COMPLEX PART OF C-PTSD

Complex trauma occurs when human relations are involved – betrayal of trust, confusion and fear.

In a toxic family it is having to walk on eggshells because of the seemingly random punishments which are generated by the issues of the parents rather than the behaviour of the children. It comes from not having control over the source of the stress, and not having anyone to help you deal with the aftermath.

As mentioned above, one way of dealing with C-PTSD is to process specific memories as an adult – this helps us overturn the feelings of being small, powerless and trapped. But this does not work so well with fear and anxiety, which the reptilian brain deals with.

Some days I experienced a feeling of dread inside without any specific memories surfacing. It was the state of expecting the future to bring bad things. It was having a generally heavy feeling inside and wanting to cry for no reason at all. This specific experience probably came from my emotional abandonment at an early age.

THE 'DISAPPEARING IDENTITY' ISSUE

Some of my C-PTSD issues had to do with meeting people. When I was prepared for an encounter I could cope. But when I was surprised I could easily lose control. It was a peculiar experience. I do not know the psychological name for it, if there is one. Perhaps you have experienced this as well. I will try to describe it below:

As a survivor I found that when I was alone I was having the most control over my mental state. I could enjoy a quality and productive time. I was okay with the things I did and who I was, and there was no judgement. I had learned to treat myself with care.

The unexpected presence of other people, however, still triggered a strong reaction of withdrawal. If I was surprised by a sudden visit, or by meeting someone on the street, I felt shaky and not in control. It was as if my identity had fled the scene and my body was left with little to control my behaviour. Not surprisingly, I ended up saying things I did not want to say, and acted in a way I did not want to act.

The unexpected presence of others was still registering as a danger. I wondered why this kept happening, and I think I found the answer.

When surprised I was trying to come across as 'normal' – I was reacting out of an old habit of putting up a front, which was meant to hide all those parts of me that I used to be ashamed of.

When I did that even as a survivor, my true identity, the person I had become because of my new outlook and knowledge, just disappeared. After such an encounter I wondered why I behaved the way I did and I had a heavy feeling in my chest. I felt as if I had somehow lost something.

It was the surprising nature of the encounter that triggered the C-PTSD and the old co-dependent behaviour.

Maybe this has happened to you too. In such moments it feels like you are drawing your responses from some barely accessible database of how confident people should behave. Of course such behaviour is not genuine. Later on you feel bad because you let yourself down yet again.

To me, it felt as though in the presence of others my personality had less 'weight', and was 'displaced' easily. I would become defensive as a reflex and not feel free to do or say what I wanted. Another default from the past – trying to justify my presence.

This type of reaction was a form of emotional dysregulation, of course. It was part of the package of growing up with dysfunction and abuse. It was a major problem during my last depressive episode, when I would get 'displaced' by others for days at a time.

I knew I was not supposed to be feeling this way anymore, but it was automatic. It felt like I could not quite 'hold' the space I was occupying. Again, it happened when I was surprised. When I was ready to socialise I was mostly fine.

In this case there was no specific memory I could process. It was a repeated injury, it was a state of mind enforced for years. It was a state of existence in which everybody else was better and more important than I was.

Well, the good thing was that my true identity came back after that; it was not permanently destroyed as the true identity of my narcissistic parent.

My present identity was who I had become as a survivor, and it included everything I had learned about mental health and about self-love, acceptance and compassion. And the most important thing I had learned was that my value did not depend on the opinion of others nor the circumstances I found myself in.

As a survivor I could be myself. But I needed to have my identity with me all the times, and this was why I had to deal with this 'disappearing identity' problem.

During such moments it was hard to do anything but get my privacy back as soon as possible. I knew it was hard to control the reptile brain, so I just let it happen and tried not to blame myself. C-PTSD is difficult to deal with and I knew I needed patience.

In general, you can do many things to make yourself a permanent occupant of your body and mind, and this follows through with the recovery process.

I had to look for solutions to the C-PTSD in order to recover completely. I will talk about these solutions a little later in the book.

ALWAYS REMEMBER HOW MUCH PROGRESS WE HAVE MADE SO FAR

Here is something very important at this stage – remembering how much progress we have already made. I have been talking about the issues I still had, but I well knew how much better my life had become.

In the past I was unable to express the pain I was in, and it was suffocating me. I was broken so badly I barely functioned. I shook at interviews and choked under pressure, I was embarrassed by who I was, and I hated myself for it. I could not look people in the eyes. Each time I tried to talk about my childhood my voice used to shake and I couldn't help bursting into tears. Now I could argue my case in a calm manner. This was amazing progress!

To be honest I struggle to find the words to describe how I used to feel because I have not felt this way for a long time.

In the last few years I have become a human being who is no longer afraid to look in the mirror. I have even started taking selfies. I wore shorts in summer and the self-hatred I used to experience was gone. I enjoyed swimming and going out in the sun. I could concentrate and learn, as well as plan for the future.

I still had issues, and those which were left were very stubborn but not nearly as bad as they used to be. However, they were preventing my full recovery.

All I had to do was to carry on adjusting the formula, using the tools I already had in a better way, and to learn new ways of coping. Just continue to get a little better each day.

...

So, let's carry on. What do we know so far about C-PTSD?

SECURE AND INSECURE ATTACHMENTS

Emotional dysregulation has a strong link to the attachment formed with the primary caregiver. According to the experts, attachment is about feeling safe and valued. The insecure connection with the caregiver translates into an insecure connection with oneself, future friends and partners. It translates into social anxiety, hypervigilance and catastrophising. It leads to depression, substance abuse, inability to concentrate, feeling damaged, and hopelessness.

All this comes from the inability to process emotions like a mentally healthy person. Processing emotions is somewhat similar to processing memories. I will summarise below:

PROCESSING EMOTIONS

So far we know plenty about dealing with emotions: do not fight them, do not retreat, just experience the emotions as deeply as you can, lean towards them, go through and to the other side. After that, apply reason and logic.

Emotions want to be acknowledged, this is their purpose. Then the brain takes on the input. By denying and mocking your emotions, the narcissistic parent devalued your personality and existence.

Not ignoring our emotions is important, we know that now. Some therapists recommend trying to turn up the frightening emotions and enjoy them as one would enjoy a thunder storm. This is a bit scary, but the fear can be turned into excitement, because the physiological basis for the two emotions is similar. And we have to acknowledge that thunderstorms exist, and they will happen once in a while. Instead of trying to hide away we may as well do the best with what we have.

I am not agreeing with this advice light-heartedly. I was someone on the edge of suicide. Back then I was trying to fight my bad feelings and I was in a very bad shape. Fighting feelings is like fighting yourself, it is not a healthy thing to do. Now I try to listen and understand my feelings, and I try to decide what is the best way to react.

Even the extreme emotions matter, like my feelings about my neighbour that I mentioned in the beginning. Yes, the feeling of anger was very intense and definitely not healthy. It was an overreaction. But it was there to tell me that I had to resolve an issue and I was not going about it the right way.

Accepting your feelings does not mean acting on them instantly, it just means acknowledging what they stand for. Naming things works. It disperses the fog. Understand what it is and what you have to do about it. Being authentic is being honest, accepting and compassionate at the same time.

Being authentic, by the way, is not about letting others know what your true feelings are. It is about accepting what is happening in your own head and in your heart, not broadcasting it. This space inside your head should be safe, because you are in charge and you answer to no one but yourself. Feel free to ask why you feel the way you feel, and give yourself an honest and helpful answer, even if it is not flattering. Care and compassion, remember. No judgment.

Example:

I had to call a hotel I had booked because I had some questions about the parking. As the receptionist picked up the phone my voice became shaky and hollow. I knew this feeling, of course. For some reason at this moment I felt like a small, dependent, scared child. Something had triggered this reaction, so I took the time to work out what it was. In this case the trigger was my grumpy husband sitting on the couch and listening to the call because he wanted to know about the parking too. I had reacted as a child to the bad mood of my husband, the same way I had reacted many times before to my parents in my family of origin.

Admitting that made me feel a bit unwell, but it was helpful. I had to face my feelings. In truth I did feel dependent on my husband. He was more confident and able to cope, and on occasions I did feel inferior to him. And, if triggered, I still felt as powerless as I did in my family of origin, though the circumstances have changed a great deal. In my marriage I was an equal partner and not the dependant I was at home. The feeling of inferiority, however, was still strong despite the new circumstances because it was my C-PTSD in action.

It was clear to me that if I wanted to be able to make phone calls like an adult, I had to find a way to deal with my C-PTSD issues.

I can hear some of you gasp 'And you are thinking about it now?' Yes, I am thinking about it after twenty years of marriage. It is not that surprising. I had reacted as a child many times before, and I had dismissed this reaction each time without facing it.

This is what the brain fog was about – ignoring most of my inconvenient feelings and senses. Instead of facing issues I was focusing on the next the steps, the next hour, the next day. The rest was sort of hazed back, and I could easily ignore and stuff back bits and pieces because I had been doing that for as long as I could remember. This is why I over-used alcohol to numb my daily experiences.

Most of the survivors of childhood abuse will be familiar with this. Part of having your brain in survival mode is being in the haze – no long term plans, just the next step. It feels like we are trapped in something sticky and it is best not to think about how we feel.

Humans are able to still function with considerable damage to the brain, just not function very well.

Back when I was writing my first CV, for example, I could not remember the names of the two schools I went to. I had studied there for years, and I could not remember the names for the life of me. And I struggled to remember the years I studied there as well. This was the brain damage caused by the major depression I suffered at university. During this period I had other strange experiences, like shaking when meeting people and blathering things I did not want to say. And this was not my last major depressive episode.

Most of the damage was reversible, it turned out. About eight years ago I came across online information about emotional abuse and narcissistic mothers, and started my recovery. Since then my concentration has improved and my interest in life has come back. I am very grateful for every bit of help I received.

Coming out of the fog happened over time, of course. For me it was experiencing a new awareness of space. It was as if a switch had flipped in my brain. Everything was where it was supposed to be – at a distance from me. The past was behind me and the future was in the future. I was present in my body and there were no other people occupying my mental space.

This was such a good feeling.

Then the fog would come again and everything would be jumbled together. Negative feelings, problems, lots of little hurdles, past and present, all these would clutter the space in my head. The presence of others would register inside my head again. It was mindboggling how much power I gave people to make me feel bad, even when they were nowhere near me.

The state of being crowded and being in a fog was just that – my damaged mind.

The good news was that I was able to experience having borders. This was progress, because with some effort I was able to prioritise my existence and clear my head. I could make the mental shift from no borders to borders. I was not able to maintain these borders all the time but I believed it was only a question of time.

Another example:

I watched *Where the Wild Things Are* recently, a well-known movie I had not seen before, and for some reason it triggered a strong emotional flashback. Ten minutes into it I was crying, and in another ten I was in such a state I was unable to stop crying.

First of all, I tried to identify the main feeling I was experiencing. It was not loneliness, it was not self-loathing, or pain, or anger, or anxiety. And it was not shame. It was an overwhelming, dark feeling, and it kept on coming and coming from a bottomless place in the heart of me.

Then I explored my reactions and where the pain was felt in my body. It was not the laboured, shame-induced cry that comes with quivering jaw and lump in the throat. It was an absolute outpouring. It was the cry of a small child, the kind that distorts the face, stretches the mouth into an arch and curves the lower lip outwards.

The emotions I was feeling were helplessness and desperation. It was a powerful experience, indeed, because it came with a sense of child-like lack of control. This was exactly what I was experiencing and finding the words to describe it was the first step to processing the flashback.

Next I tried to attach the experience to a specific time and memory in order to understand it intellectually. A few memories came to my mind, too many, in fact. Crying as a lonely child, at night as a teenager, and when I was in a hospital.

So, there was not just one memory. It more of an overwhelming feeling I had experienced at different stages of my life.

The last step was going as far back as I could and focusing on the earlier versions of me experiencing this feeling. I started processing by letting the child know that the future was going to be okay, and letting her know who I had become now. The child understood what was happening, of course, because I understood.

This shifted the trauma that was formed back to those days and a strange change of perception occurred. I could remember the pain I was in a minute ago but I did not feel like crying because the experience was from another time.

When I processed feelings this way I knew the process worked because I felt a definite sense of relief afterwards. I think the key was searching for the source of the pain without fear of what I might find. I had embraced my worst moments as an important part of me.

In this case, the next day I was able to go back to the movie and enjoy it without falling apart.

CHILDREN OF NARCISSISTS AND RECOVERY

Which brings me to another important question, and maybe you are wondering the same thing.

The term 'recovery' implies that one goes back to a better state of mind, to being mentally healthy and functioning well. But what about children of narcissistic parents? The assault on our personalities began so early, what do we really have to go back to?

I will give an example of what I mean:

I had a very early memory that stood out because it involved a very unusual, transparent umbrella with cartoon pictures of the sun on it. My aunt brought the umbrella to me as a gift. She tried to give it to me at a family gathering and I could not take it. I remember standing away and having an overwhelming and paralysing feeling of confusion.

First, the umbrella was so beautiful and exotic it was clearly not for me. Second, I had no clue what I had to do in return. I knew I had to 'repay' my upkeep with good behaviour, but the umbrella was too much. I feared I could not perform to expectations and give whatever was expected from me in return, because I did not know what that was.

I was four- or five-years old and self-abandonment was already happening at this early stage – I thought I did not deserve beautiful things and the image I had of myself was already negative. Most of my effort was focused on my parents and on how to avoid being rejected. This behaviour was rewarded by my narcissistic mother, and people-pleasing was already a part of my identity.

So, it was a fair question. Who was I before the erosion of my identity started? Knowing that the lack of empathy is what defines a narcissistic mother, it started as soon as I was born. Maybe some of you are asking the same thing.

The answer I could come up with was as follows: I was someone who could recall this memory and understand what was happening and why it was wrong. Some of my essence, or healthy ego, had survived. I had the ability to separate that authentic sense of self from the damage caused by others.

It could be because I stayed with my grandparents often and they were wonderful to me. Maybe it was about school and my abilities there. Maybe it was the books I read. I was more than a product of my mother's narcissism and my father's anger. I had good memories and valuable experiences, they were just overshadowed by the prevalence of the negative attitude of my parents towards me.

I think if we have made it so far into recovery, we have enough to work with. For me it was becoming easier and easier to flip the switch and experience borders and unconditional self-love.

The things we did not get to learn as children were basic and simple, and some people may ask what took us so long to understand things as simple as borders and self-respect. Well, there are adults who cannot read because they were not taught how to.

Common things are not so simple if there is a serious deviation from the norm.

Adults can learn to read. And it is possible to change the wiring of the brain. Remember how much progress we have made so far? Becoming a survivor has taken off much of the crushing load, now we just have to deal with the few remaining issues.

...

Now, back to C-PTSD and the physiological responses that were stubborn and hard to shift – tension, heartbeat, irregular breathing. My dysregulated reactions seemed to be set by surprise, loud noises, door-slamming and other physical triggers, and resulted in sleepless nights, difficulty concentrating and bad moods. Fear can be about the future, fear of people, and fear of failure, yet it felt like fear for my life.

You probably have noticed that I am still trying to use reason and logic even though I am talking about C-PTSD. Reason and logic work well when it comes to dealing with the resulting overreaction from C-PTSD. But what could I do to stop those overreactions happening in the first place?

Good questions. No easy answers. Fear and pain, they are such important aspects of survival, and the reptilian brain responsible for that is very reactive.

LOOKING FOR SOLUTIONS TO C-PTSD

There was an abundance of information out there about healing from C-PTSD. It came from doctors, therapist and survivors. The problem was, however, that there so much information, and I was not sure what was the best way to approach my remaining problems.

After considering what I had read about it, I came to the conclusion I needed to do more things practically, rather than trying to understand the psychology behind C-PTSD.

I had to make a consistent practical effort to improve my mental state. I needed to make an effort and do all those exercises I had read about and tried only once or twice. I had to do the work.

And again, there are many practical exercises suggested for combating C-PTSD and turning off the amygdalae. All of them sounded like good ideas: breathing, meditating, challenging your reactions by asking questions, tapping or Emotional Freedom Techniques, mindfulness, writing down your fears every day, befriending fear, and so on.

In the midst of all that information I found the most common denominators – breathing, mindfulness and affirmations.

BREATHING TECHNIQUES

Breathing appeared to be one of the most important strategies everyone was talking about. And there were many breathing techniques I came across that were quite similar. I will briefly mention two examples:

Two by six by eight – breathe in for two seconds, hold for six, and release slowly for eight seconds.

Square breathing – breathe in for four seconds, hold in for four seconds, and breathe out for four seconds. Then hold for four seconds, and do the same thing again four times.

Such breathing exercises seem to be very important for avoiding panic attacks and overreactions, for calming down and improving one's concentration.

I came across a meditation technique based simply on observing your breathing. It is about taking deep breaths and releasing them slowly while staying focused on your breathing for as long as you can.

One technique worth mentioning helps with the prevention of panic attacks, but I found it was good for releasing tension when I was so overwhelmed nothing else worked. It is as follows: First, take a deep breath. Tighten your body, the whole body, every single muscle you can at the same time, from the tip of your nose to your toes. Just do it as hard as you can, push your limits just for a few seconds. Then breathe out and relax all the muscles.

This helps because sometimes we do not even realise our muscles are tight, not until we think about it consciously.

All these techniques have one thing in common – breathing in slowly and deeply, holding, then releasing the air very slowly.

Breathing properly is very important, most sources agree on that. Abuse victims tend to hold their breath without realizing it and it starves the blood of oxygen. It has to do with the constant state of anticipating trouble in dysfunctional families. The problem with children of narcissists is that our abnormal breathing patterns have become a normal state and are hard to catch when they occur.

I knew I was guilty of that, and my breathing was shallow and erratic at times. I caught myself tensing my stomach muscles as well. And the best way to turn the stress, and turn off the amygdala that was producing it, was to breathe properly.

POSITIVE AFFIRMATIONS

Positive affirmations are very important for changing the negative image the narcissistic parent mirrored back to us. A major step to thriving is changing the story, the way survivors think of themselves.

I have used affirmations at different times in my life. They helped me in the short run when I was relatively well, but during my depressive episodes they stopped working. Later, I understood this was because I was using affirmations that were not realistic, such as 'I am great', or 'I am special'.

'Special' is not a word I like much now, because narcissists are addicted to being special, and we, their children, paid the price for that. As I mentioned in the first book, the narcissistic parent took away the healthy narcissism we needed to protect our values, needs, and self-image.

Positive and believable affirmations work well to override the default settings of feeling subnormal. They work as long as they come with understanding and compassion for who you really are, including both your weaknesses and strengths.

Sometimes it is more beneficial to use words that reflect how you feel, yet which are positive and hopeful. Something like, 'Right now I feel sad and damaged, but that's okay, because I love myself unconditionally.'

Of course, you can find what works for you. I found the affirmation that really resonated with me in a video by Pia Mellody, an expert on addiction and emotional dysfunction. She teaches that self-esteem is not a scale that slides up or down, but something that is either on or off. The worth of a person is a given, it is not something that increases or decreases according to outside influences.

The affirmation that resonated with me was, 'I matter as I am.' Very simple and very effective. I do believe self-esteem should be unconditional. This is why I matter as I am, whether I am ill or healthy, rich or poor, whether I succeed or fail. I matter because I exist.

MINDFULNESS

I mention this last, but it is very, very important to the recovery from C-PTSD. Mindfulness is an excellent tool for reducing chronic stress and calming the dysregulated brain.

However, it is important for more than that. It is about bringing the mind into the present, where it should be. Mindfulness is the ability to be connected with your feelings and needs, and to feel in control of both your mind and body.

There are different techniques for practising mindfulness:

You can take an object, for example, and look at it. If you really look at it, as if you have never seen anything like that before, then you are likely to experience mindfulness – being in the present with all your senses. Breathing or counting can be used as well.

Being present in the moment feels like being comfortably in the back of your head. Both being present in the moment and feeling present in your body are where you are supposed to be. Then the personal boundaries become clear and you are able to see the past and the future in perspective.

I do apologise if this sounds silly or patronizing. It is obvious one should be in one's head, but I had considerable problems doing exactly that. It does sound daft, but it probably sounds much dafter to those who had never been 'out of their heads'. It has to do with our disorder and the anxiety that comes with it.

Think what happens when you are experiencing tension and flashbacks – your mind is skittish and it feels like your emotions exist outside of the control of your mind. But if you can calm down and be present, your thoughts and feelings go back inside your head and you are able to make decisions and assess the situation accurately.

This is the best way I can explain the shift to a healthier perception. Thriving would mean doing exactly that, effortlessly and at all times.

The next big question – how do I use these techniques to help my C-PTSD?

PRACTICAL EXERCISES

So far I had decided that I needed to do practical exercises to improve my mental health and to calm down the amygdalae. This is why I chose only three steps, to simplify and make the exercises easy to follow through.

I got a beeper app for my mobile phone, one I could set to beep at any time-interval to remind me to do my exercises. I set the alarm on the hour and, when I could, I changed it to every ten minutes. I wanted to repeat the new routine as often as I could.

I decided to keep it as simple as possible.

SIMPLE THREE STEPS ROUTINE

STEP 1

Relax: Take a deep breath, hold it, then let it out very slowly. This will bring me back into my body. Repeat if needed.

STEP 2

Say: 'I matter as I am.'

Say it gently, assertively and calmly.

STEP 3

Mindfulness: Experience mindfulness. Become aware of my surroundings, my existence and my presence. Notice sounds, colours, feelings. Experience my body, try to detect any tension and discomfort, then soothe it.

...

This was my three-steps plan. It was a simple plan, something I could stick with even if my concentration was not good.

And, indeed, I did manage to stick with it. The mobile application allowed me to change the sound of the alarm. I wanted to practice these three simple exercises until they became truly entrenched in my brain. At first they could become a ritual, then a routine, and then a habit – an automatic reaction and second nature.

When there were people around I would switch the phone to vibrate mode, and I carried it strapped to my arm. I wanted to deal with the C-PTSD and I was determined to change. I expected it was going to take at least three months. Practice and repetition seemed to be the key.

SURPRISING SETBACK

After the first month of using this three-step exercise something unexpected happened. I had a very strong emotional flashback.

It was a Sunday and I was in the park on a sunny winter's day. There were many people there, families and kids, and the trigger, I believe, was the winter sun shining into my eyes at a particular angle.

It was a flashback I had experienced before and it was about the winter weekends with my father, when I was a child. The experience was more like a punishment that a day out. It was an awkward and unpleasant experience. My father was silent and sulky and I was tense and unhappy. The way there he didn't talk, just cleared his throat at intervals as if he was about to say something. I don't know whether he could not be bothered or he had no idea what to say.

Once we arrived he tried to teach me how to ski by shouting commands and making disappointed grunts when I fell down. I was tired, my father was frustrated with me, the sun was in my eyes, my nose was running, and I was miserable.

As the day progressed the bitter lump in my throat grew, and the sunlight reflected from the snow made my eyes water. When my father noticed he made disappointed grunts because he thought I was crying. Then I did start crying and my disgrace was complete. We went back home in silence. I could not wait for the weekend to be over. It was a very unpleasant memory and I clearly remembered the feeling of being humiliated and tearful.

So, on a sunny Sunday, a year into my recovery, the brain neurons that were connected with this memory fired together and gave me that very same experience. I felt the pain in my throat as intensely as I did when I was a child, and the tears were pushing to get out in the same unstoppable way. I was physically unable to stop my lip and jaw from trembling.

I had regressed to a child again, being trapped in an unpleasant situation with a lump in my throat and tears just about to pour out. As if no time had passed at all, the shame burned my eyes and the choking feeling of humiliation was as overwhelming as it had been back then.

It was an epic flashback. It was almost like a panic attack in the way it came over me and I was not able to reason it away. The memory was very much happening in the 'now'.

Luckily I was not far from home. I made it back and collapsed crying. It was a major setback, but even as I was crying at home I managed to employ what I knew about dealing with flashbacks. As soon as I could I wrote this experience down. Every detail of the memory I could think of; I wrote it in in an erratic manner, with disconnected sentences, using the very words that came to my mind.

Instead of pulling away I went right in, as deep as I could, and let myself feel my feelings without trying to put any stops to the experience. No more twitching and hiding. I went into the pain, turned it into a thunderstorm and appreciated the force of it.

I did it purposefully and without fear, and with the knowledge that it had happened when I was a child. I felt what I felt without fear. I cried and let the pain out. I did the very opposite of what I did as a humiliated child – trying to contain and keep the pain inside of me. I found the depths of my misery and went right in there, looking for the worst of it.

That worked. I came down.

After that I took a deep breath and summoned my mind back into my body. It was the child inside me that had experienced what I felt. And though it had caught me by surprise and affected me in such a powerful way, I knew what to do.

After I came down the older part of me started analysing the experience.

PROCESSING THE MEMORY

There was so much more around this memory that I could heal. The flashback had as much to do with the happy families I saw in the park that Sunday as with the angle of the winter sun.

As an adult I could ask questions I did not ask as a child. Like, why did my father choose me? Why didn't he teach my brother how to ski? Why didn't he go with friends? Obviously, because my brother refused to go with him, and my father had no friends. My father was not pleasant company and there was no one else willing to put up with him. He expected me to fill that gap and it was not within my abilities to do that.

My father was in charge, it was his lack of social skills that made the trip a disaster. Yet I was the one feeling responsible for disappointing him because I was at the receiving end of his frustration. I felt extremely tired, physically and emotionally.

As an adult I understood that my father's lack of basic communication skills became my burden. The toxic shame I had in me internalised his behaviour as my inability to resolve the situation.

All this was too much for a child; it overwhelmed me and I could not cope. As an adult I had an idea how to cope. First of all, take the burden off me and give it back to where it came from, and second, treat myself with the compassion, acceptance and love I never got as a child.

My father exhibited a very common behaviour of toxic parents – when I made a mistake he instantly reacted with anger and annoyance as if my mistake had affected him directly. In this respect my father was an enmeshed parent because he was embarrassed by any mistakes or blunders as if they were about him.

As a survivor I understood well what happened and why it affected me badly. It was a powerful memory, no doubt, and it made me feel like a scared child in my grown body.

On the bright side, I managed to process it within two hours. The adult in me employed all the compassion and acceptance I could master to convince the child I used to be that the toxic shame I carried was not mine.

THE LITTLE PRINCE

The Little Prince is an emotionally-charged little book by Antoine de Saint-Exupéry. It was first published in 1943 and is still relevant somehow. As a child I came across it in the school library. I was so taken by the book I asked my father a question that arose from the book. I got back an expression of disgust that reduced me to nothing. He had read the book, he knew the answer, and he was shocked and disappointed that I did not.

Coincidently, the essence of the book was about the connection between an adult and a child, based on empathy and emotional exchange. I cried while reading this book as a child, without knowing where the pain came from.

I did know now – it came from the lack of such connection. It was about what I did not get, and what I needed as a child to feel okay – validation and guidance based on empathy, closeness, positive regard, and love.

Recently I read the book again. This time I had the emotional maturity to appreciate the impact of the book without feeling the pain and desperation I did as a child. And this was another small step towards recovery.

EXPERIENCING THE SHIFTING OF THE PAIN IN THE BODY

Something I have noticed as a survivor was that the generalised anxiety I felt was now in the middle of my body – in my stomach, under my ribcage and in the heart. It was much more bearable. It was still heavy, but it was not the intense choking pain in the throat I felt when I was young.

It might be bit literal but it makes sense – the pain in the throat was an early pain, it was a choking and nameless pain. I went through this misery again and again without being able to see a way out. I had no voice, no ability to speak up for myself. This is why the pain I was feeling was a lump in my throat.

After the healing process began the pain moved to under my ribcage, but mostly it was just sitting in the gut as a low-level tension or a fear reaction. I had spoken my truth, and my adult brain had acquired the ability to process memories and understand the importance of self-care. I had processed many of my experiences but some trauma was still left unresolved, mostly C-PTSD related.

And this was the very thing I was trying to fix when I had this major flashback. So, what on earth happened?

My simple three-steps program had managed to trigger a memory that was so vivid and overwhelming, and I could not help wondering why I had regressed so far.

THE REASONS FOR THE FLASHBACK

I have to admit that I was taken aback. Maybe breathing so deeply and so often was unnecessary and harmful, and doing it had made my C-PTSD symptoms worse. This was one possible answer.

As you can guess, making up my own exercises was not such a good idea. It is best to follow exercises designed and recommended by professionals. My program created an issue rather than solving anything.

Ideally everyone would have a good professional therapist and not make up things on the go. For various reasons this is not always possible. Anyway, my experiment was not all in vain. As well as realising this routine was not helpful, I found something else that was not very helpful, something very important – trying hard does not work for adult children of covert narcissists.

WHY TRYING HARD DOES NOT WORK

A thought occurred to me about a week later and it felt like a piece of the puzzle had fallen into place.

My major flashback was a result of being determined to succeed in my recovery in a way that was not about compassion and acceptance. I had put pressure on myself to finally fix my C-PTSD, or else!

Trying hard is something children of covert narcissists know about. I am talking about trying hard to please, to be liked, to achieve, to appear okay. Trying hard to impress and to succeed despite our skittish minds and our lack of ability to cope.

I tried hard to function, with progressively worsening mental health, through my teenage and adulthood years, and it was an agonizing journey of feeling and performing worse and worse.

Trying hard was a big part of my life. It was a response to growing up with criticism and with the constant fear of further devaluation. It was a struggle just to stay in the same place my narcissistic mother put me in – waiting for validation and not getting it. Familiar? Maybe you also grew up thinking if you just tried harder things would be different.

Trying hard has an element of desperation and with that comes a high level of anxiety and panic. So, I was trying to 'get rid' of the consequences of that very affliction by trying hard. There was something very wrong about that, and something very familiar at the same time.

It was like trying to ski when my body felt like jelly, or trying so hard to be liked when I was sliding down the social ladder. But instead of letting go, I kept on trying harder with my jaw and fists clenched because it felt like my life depended on it. You get the picture.

Trying hard, as I found the hard way, was a trigger. Basically I fell into an old trap, and my flashback reminded me of that pretty quickly. Being so determined to get results I threw myself into it with the eager desire to prove I could get better. Even if I was trying to prove it to myself, it was the wrong approach. Trying hard was the very reason I suffered from adrenal fatigue for years. The harder I tried, the more likely it was that I was going to fail. Trying hard was associated with being overwhelmed, alone and fearful.

Unwittingly, by trying hard to make myself better I had returned to this very unstable state of mind. Trying hard was not the right approach and I think my mind rebelled against going down this road again, and reacted with a strong flashback.

THE RIGHT APPROACH

I did not have to prove I could get better to myself or to anyone.

Can you tell the difference between 'failing to thrive', and 'not being there yet'? Not being there yet is an observation. Failing to thrive is a self-proclaimed defeat and a way of being your own worst enemy.

I had to go back to feeling compassion and acceptance, and back to appreciating myself in the present, and being in my body and in my own head. It was a far better and far more productive way to be. I had to make the past a comfortable part of who I was.

DO NOT FIGHT YOURSELF!

If there is one piece of advice you take away from this book, I hope that this is it. Do not fight yourself. Do not repeat my mistake and put pressure and a timeline on your recovery. When we do that we get stuck deeper.

There are better ways to get things done.

BACK TO THREE STEPS AND DEALING WITH COMPLEX-PTSD

So I learned something from my ill-fated three-steps exercise.

I had clearly misused the techniques of breathing, mindfulness and affirmation, but that did not mean they were not important. They are, in fact, excellent tools for dealing with C-PTSD. They are what you need when your frontal lobe is struggling to override the reactions of the reptilian brain.

And there were many positives to reflect on.

I did not get angry with myself for failing. And I did not give up. I just had to change the three-steps plan.

The episode I experienced did not take days to process, as it used to. I processed the winter sun memory, went through it and came out the other side. Doing this was important for my mental health. And after the storm subsided I felt contented with who I had become – someone capable of handling issues. And I knew the next time I would handle such surprise attacks even better.

So I brushed myself off, re-traced my steps, and tried to use the three steps in a recommended way.

NEW USE FOR THE THREE TOOLS

Breathing deeply, mindfulness, and affirmations work well. All I had to do was use them in a better way.

Step one, for example, was to start the day with positivity, with affirmations that reminded me of my intrinsic worth. The second step was to practise mindfulness during the day. And the last step was to do breathing exercises before going to sleep.

Again, easy to remember and I did not need a phone reminder. I did the exercises without pressure.

MINDFULNESS

Mindfulness heals that very sense of 'displacement' I mentioned, and I will try to explain why.

The idea of mindfulness is to experience observing without thinking or judging, and without being under any pressure to do anything about the things you are observing.

To practice mindfulness just empty your mind, observe for a period of time, become aware you are observing, and stay in that state without engaging. You can focus on an object, or a sound, or a feeling. Stay focused on one of these for as long as you can, than move onto something else. Use your senses, not your thinking brain. Capture a sound, for example, and just focus on it. Or feel a spot in your body.

For me it is easier with an object. Looking at a pen on my desk, for example. It is not pretty, or ugly, easy to write with or not, it is not cheap or expensive. Looking at it is not about what it is or what it does. The pen is simply an object that exists in front of me and that has nothing to do with me for the moment. I am only looking at it as if I have never seen such an object before. I do not name or think about the physical attributes of the pen. I am focusing my senses on observing it but not on thinking about it.

After a while things around it become fuzzy, and the object appears to stand out and I experience a definite sense of being present, of sensing my own existence at that moment. This is experiencing mindfulness – I become aware that I am staring at a pen at this very moment. I am sitting right here and the pen is in front of me and I am looking at the pen.

That is experiencing awareness. You don't have to do anything with it, just let it be. The idea is to disengage that relentless, panicky, always judging and thinking part of the brain that causes fear and anxiety. That can be done by channelling your full attention onto only one thing. The key is observing and becoming aware without judging.

The 'grey rock', 'observe but not absorb', uses this ability of the mind to disconnect from something and connect to something else without having to commit emotionally or intellectually.

Mindfulness is the skill of not engaging.

During my breakdown I was unable to stop engaging, and that wore me down so badly I nearly gave up. I remember the feeling of being under attack by noises around me, by people and their agendas, by bad things in the news, tragic movie plots, ugly politics, dogs barking, the wind blowing, by my own negativity and ineptitude. My borders had disintegrated and I was about to be torn apart.

Disengaging is the opposite of enmeshment. It is about giving yourself a break from all those attacks on your senses.

It is helpful, and it is worth the time you invest, to learn mindfulness. For example, if you focus on a sensation in your body, do not try to understand it. Just observe it.

As another example, I learned to switch off topics such as politics at will. At one moment I could feel frustrated by something as if it was inside of me, and the next moment this was a problem outside of me and completely irrelevant to my wellbeing at that instant.

The skill to do that came with learning to observe and disengage. It works the same whether you are looking at a pen, or at a person, or at a geo-political conflict.

Mindfulness is good for changing core beliefs that are damaging to you. That is because mindfulness helps you to stay in your body and in the now and this allows you to develop boundaries and a sense of self.

OTHER TECHNIQUES FOR COMBATING C-PTSD

Gratitude is a positive emotion. It is uplifting and feels like a warmth in the centre of the body. It is about focusing on everything good that is in our lives, and we often ignore the good because of our survival-focused brains.

There is plenty to be thankful for, always. Having food, a home, having eyes and ears and hands, and internet access, and so on. Some of the things I came up with were: sleeping in a bed with clean sheets, or just the fact I had a warm bed to go to. Or having a shower. I was thankful for my husband, for my hobbies, for a good book, an interesting nature documentary or an afternoon out. I was thankful for the leaves on the trees. If you have a favourite TV program, make watching it a special event.

You may have noticed the things I listed are to do with the environment. It is important to be grateful for who you are as well, for having that little light inside of you, for having a warm heart, for being a survivor.

Be grateful for anything you choose. The little things, like the sun outside and a tasty sandwich. And the big things, of course. I am grateful I survived.

All of the above help to create a space inside your head that is pleasant and safe, so your mind would rather stay there instead of going backwards and forwards restlessly, looking for bad things and danger.

I learned to appreciate the things that give me comfort. My computer, for example, was a constant source of information and entertainment. And, very important – I was grateful I was on the path to recovery. My brain was starting to work again and I wanted to learn new things. Without a doubt, this was a great improvement.

...

Grounding is another way to be present, similar to mindfulness, but it is about visualising that you have roots, feeling your feet on the ground, feeling your own body as a mighty tree. It is a way of experiencing being in your body and in the moment.

There are other ways, like saying your name and where you are, noticing what you touch and how it feels, listening to the sounds, noticing the colours and textures of the objects around you. Using all your senses to experience your reality and be present.

Whatever you do, notice when you are comfortable and safe. Slow down and enjoy such moments. But do it gently. Don't try too hard to experience positivity and safety. If you try to force yourself to feel these things, it will not work.

SOCIAL ANXIETY TECHNIQUE

There are many techniques to help us combat our many issues. One worth mentioning is a technique for dealing with social anxiety.

When being uncomfortable talking to people, make the effort to fix your attention on them and their behaviour. It is what most people do, but our dysfunction compels us otherwise.

If you manage to keep your attention on them for at least a while, you may notice other people are just people and they have their own issues.

DISTRACTION TECHNIQUES

After having the surprising winter sun flashback I had a few more 'tremors' before I got back on track with my recovery.

Processing memories and flashbacks by re-experiencing the trauma is fine in the safety of your home. But what about when you are away from home and in the presence of other people?

It happened to me, and this is how I discovered that I could use distraction techniques that I could not use as a victim because they were not adequate for the amount of pain I was in.

The idea was to keep my reactions to the flashback until I was in a safe place. As a survivor I had a healthier brain in general, and this is why the techniques that just annoyed me in the past worked rather well this time.

Counting backwards from a hundred is an example of such a technique. Or trying to say the alphabet backwards. Another one is practicing the multiplication tables in your head. It helps if you are bad at math. It worked well for me – it took all my brain power to do some simple calculations.

...

Once you are in a safe place it is best to let your emotions out and process them. A good practice is to pay attention to the physical manifestation of the emotions in the body. We know that negative emotions like fear, shame or pain are experienced in a very physical way. I learned to pay attention to where such feelings were in my body and simply acknowledge and honour them.

I was also trying to work out where the emotions came from. Did they come from recalling past experiences, or something recent, or for no other reason but my over-reacting limbic system?

Most people can do this without thinking. But individuals with C-PTSD have to make an effort. And this is relevant to many other things we didn't get to learn while growing up, such as what is our personal space.

SET A PERSONAL SPACE

If you wonder what that is, stretch your arms and spin around. This is your personal space and no one else is entitled to it. Even if people want to kiss you as a greeting, this is not okay if you are not okay with it. Does it feel okay? Ask yourself that. And if it does not, just let the other know you are not a hugger. Don't let others get away with forcing their ways on you.

When someone uninvited is in your personal space it feels wrong. This is a basic self-care strategy. Most adults know that, but children of narcissists have some growing up to do. As a child my reaction was to freeze, and later in life I would ignore violations of my space just to be nice and 'accommodate' the ways of others, because I felt less important.

Borders come with a healthy state of mind, and that, of course, means thriving.

MORE ON HOW TO DEAL WITH FEELINGS

Pay attention to how you feel and acknowledge it. Ask yourself, 'Why do I feel so angry, or frustrated?' Oh, I did not sleep well, or that guy on a bike tried to run me over, or that thing is going badly. I just acknowledge the feeling and why it is there.

It sounds very basic and simple, but the brain of a child of narcissists is conditioned to ignore and bury the bad things inside because of the insinuation that acknowledging a problem is failing somehow.

And crying, crying is good. During my depressive episodes crying was an issue, and this was a sign my mind could not regulate emotions and function properly. Crying is like an emotional shower. This is not self-hatred, it is cleansing. Allow yourself to cry if you feel like it.

There is nothing wrong with being sad for a while either, as long as this does not last long. (Two weeks of feeling down is a sign of depression, according to medical advice.)

Experiencing fear or sadness has nothing to do with not loving yourself. You can love yourself even if you are feeling sad, scared, mad, abandoned or lonely. This is why it is called unconditional self-love. It is the feeling of unconditional support and respect no matter what happens to you at that moment.

This is basically how we managed to become survivors – by deciding to treat ourselves with love and respect, in the opposite way our narcissistic parents did.

Do not try to force bad feelings out or they will fight back. It is better to acknowledge and experience them until they subside. Do it with compassion and an acceptance of yourself and what you feel.

We might be little speckles in the universe but we decide what our worth and our values are. We have the consciousness to do so.

LOOKING FROM A DISTANCE

I was getting very good at this specific technique. It was about looking at my life from a distance. If you zoom out far enough, a lifetime is just a blink. Dysfunction went generations back into my family. Being born into it was not a choice, but breaking out was something to be proud of. And if you zoom out far enough this whole planet is a blue ball in space and most of our troubles are insignificant. That's getting a perspective.

But aside from those moments of contemplation, this technique is about looking at yourself from above – it is about observing how you behave, as well as observing others in a detached way. The idea is to be able to turn off that intense emotional self-involvement as well as to detach from the world around us.

If we can master the ability to switch on and off that very ability to emphasise and feel, the benefits are great. We can use our sensitivity as a power without being drained.

This technique uses elements of the mindfulness technique as well as visualization. Just imagine your mind leaving your body and hovering above you in whatever shape or manner you want. I am talking about leaving the body on purpose, not in the frightened C-

PTSD manner we have done so many times before. We want to control that ability.

If you can stay above your body you can easily move out into space, or back in time. Perception, it is all there is. Perception is a way of looking at reality, and we have to break the narcissistic spell and the learned helplessness we acquired during childhood. No matter how powerful those early memories are, as humans we can think and adapt, and this is an amazing evolutionary advance.

AUTHENTIC VERSUS GOOD

Learning about healthy and unhealthy behaviours helped me make progress with my recovery.

I had to face my shortcomings with an open mind. I used to think that being good was a quality that gave me some worth. I used to think of it as my saving grace – I was a failure, but I was a good person, and that was something to hold on to. It wasn't, of course.

The old 'good' was induced by the demands of the narcissistic parent for an obliging source of supply, and had nothing to do with the positive meaning of the world. The 'good girl' my mother wanted would put others first, did not argue, did not demand attention, acknowledged my mother's importance, did not trouble her with problems, and loved her with the neediness of a child. The reward for being 'good' was having a mother, and as a child my personality formed around this need. The punishment, of course, was an instant withdrawal of love.

For example, I thought of myself as a nature lover to such a degree I could be standing in a field of flowers and be reluctant to pick one because in my head that equated with destroying beautiful things.

This seemingly positive attitude was in fact unhealthy. When I was out in nature I could appreciate the beauty but the source was external and temporary. I came back home and the peace in my heart was gone. It was a sort of wishful thinking – if I love all living things I will get some love in return. In fact, it is the other way around – one has to receive love to give love.

In my mind, consciously or not, I was expecting some sort of universal reward for the good people. This was a very co-dependent way of thinking, expecting that if I was good I would get good things coming. This is not the case, in life or in nature. In this respect being good was a bargaining chip with which I wanted to become worthy by giving so much worth to something beautiful.

In another respect, being nice to people was simply being terrified of conflict and of displeasing. I did not speak my mind and I had abandoned my values, personality and interests. I had such a fragile sense of self that any criticism could hurt me. This was my early childhood programming driven by fear and shame.

I am repeating something I have said many times before. Yet, in this context, it is about understanding how wrong the old 'good girl' was from the start – quiet, conscientious, pleasing. It was more of an induced mental state than a genuine quality of character.

The need to be seen as good had become one of my pushbuttons. When I was called bad I felt diminished. This was a problem, because I reacted to the accusations like a scared child. Adults are supposed to self-reference, but dysfunctional families do not allow children to grow up, because it threatens the top position of the parents.

To get better I had to face my false image, and that kind of honesty was not easy. I was a little reluctant to accept that a big part of my character was false. Luckily I was prepared to change.

THE GOOD AND BAD LABEL

Part of growing up is understanding that 'good' and 'bad' are labels anyone can apply for their own benefit. You can choose to ignore the opinions of others; it is a very simple concept.

I know these are just words, but in my journey of recovery I found well-worded messages to be helpful. Narcissistic abuse is about smoke and mirrors, there is a great deal of confusion, internal bruising, unspoken condemnation and head games. Those indirect messages create a great deal of damage. And the opposite is true, clear messages help clear the clutter in my brain.

So how do we become authentic humans? Below are some rules I made for myself, maybe they will resonate with you:

HOW TO BE AUTHENTIC

Stop trying to be seen and acknowledged as 'good' is a good start. You don't have to be liked or to be nice to have a nice day.

You have to be contented with your actions and values. You know when you are nice, not someone else. Separate your interests from the interests of other people.

If you are not sure what to say or do, pause before you make a decision. First and always check with yourself, with your values, wishes and wants. When you are being authentic you feel in sync with your actions. Even if things don't work out at the end, that is fine, because you have given it your best effort. This is all you can do. The rest is often down to chance.

WHAT TO WATCH FOR

The other things we have to watch for are the leftovers from our co-dependent conditioning that have become a part of our behaviour.

As an adult, for example, it is having to justify who you are and what you stand for, but not expecting it from others, or not asking them back the same questions they ask you. Why not? This is so wrong, and this is how I used to behave for decades. Think about it; you have all the right to ask the same questions they ask you. Or to not answer, of course.

Other behaviours to watch out for are the old co-dependent reactions of having to answer questions, or answer the door, or pick up the phone, or take action immediately. The old me, for example, was not entitled to make others wait even when there was a good reason for it. Having to answer promptly was part of the self-defence when you were dependent on unpredictable parents. It should not be a part of the adult you.

Growing up is hard, and it is not easy when you have to grow up later in life. But it can be done. I believe I have made so much progress already.

RULES OF AUTHENTIC BEHAVIOUR

I will go over some of the important points again, because they will help us make our way in life as mature people.

Being authentic does not mean that you should automatically behave as you feel. If you are having a bad day you still have to be polite, for example. You are entitled to your true feelings about someone, yet you don't have to share that with them. This is for our own sakes, and for our benefit. Always showing how we feel is showing that we have no borders.

I know this is simple, but I memorised all the rules so they will just pop-up in my mind when the occasion arises and I will just stick with them.

ALWAYS BE POLITE

Approach everyone in a polite and nice way. It costs nothing but it is such an important thing. It is like wearing a protective coat. Being consistently polite protects you much better than being angry and reactive. A polite but firm 'no' is very effective.

DO NOT RAISE YOUR VOICE

Be assertive when you have to but keep your voice level. Do not mirror the moods of others. When someone raises their voice at you, do not do the same.

Certain people may try to get into your space, push you and provoke you. Do not react in the angry way you feel you should. Honouring your emotions is acting in your best interests.

If you feel you should, move away physically. Turn away. Do not answer personal questions. Say, 'That is a very personal question.' Say it with a smile, that is very important, or start asking them a lot of questions instead. Whatever works.

Other useful phrases to help you finish a conversation with unpleasant or abusive people: 'Let's agree to disagree'; 'I am sorry you feel that way'; and my favourite, 'Excuse me, I really have to go now. Goodbye.'

Enough about predators and toxic people, let's talk about the good people in this world.

THE GOOD PEOPLE

Now I ask for a little patience. I know that what I am going to say might surprise you at first.

The good people, we know they are out there. They exist, and it is wonderful to have them around. Your boss might be one. Or someone you want to make friends with. Or someone you are already friends with and you want to fight their fight.

The good people are wonderful. People who create, fight for good causes, make good things happen. They are the ones who stop this world from going down like a lead balloon.

By all means, like them, appreciate them, help them, but you need to have borders with them as much as with anyone because they will not make you feel better. They do not have magic powers. Trying to please them is just falling into the old trap but with a twist, because you really want to please the good people.

I noticed I 'lost' my identity so much more easily with good people than with predators. I empathised so easily and willingly with them and everything they stood for. I used to shake on their behalf, feel their pain, be happy when they won and be disappointed when they lost.

This was practising emotional dysregulation. There is no positive emotional dysregulation, I don't think so.

Some things to note about this concept, if you think you identify with it:

The enmeshment is in your head, not in theirs. This is why you have to make sure you are present in your body. This is why they survive and you sink, and it is not because they wish you ill.

Good people will not take from you on purpose; you will simply give everything away and be left drained all the same. Think about your experiences in the past and you might see that pattern happening as often as being drained by predators. This is because with the enmeshment you are channelling their life energy but paying for it later. Living through others is not a healthy state of being.

What can you do instead?

Nothing. Don't try to fight their fights or impress them. You can be on their team without becoming emotionally enmeshed, and this is possible if you have good borders. Being strong is being on your own side, first and always. And from that strong place of existence you can choose to be there for the good people and make good things happen as well.

Trying to hold on to good people, as proven many times before, will not keep you afloat. Only being your own person will. I talked about it in the first book, about trying to please and achieving the very opposite.

The point I am making is that children of narcissists have to learn to separate emotionally both from the good and the bad in the same way, from both the toxic and the lovely people. This is what having your identity is about – a state of serenity that does not come from others.

This, by the way, refers to your loved ones as well. Yes, I know, this is a bit of a shock to the old co-dependent system, but that's what we want to change.

For example, my husband was one of the reasons I kept going back to my default no border settings, from trying to please him to feeling his feelings. I kept linking my worth to his happiness the way I was trained to in my family of origin.

The reason for this was my personality disorder, of course. It was the familiar, unhealthy, co-dependent habit of doing everything possible to make the other comfortable without asking them what they needed or why, and then expecting they will make you comfortable and take care of you in turn.

That, of course, was not being authentic. It was trying to get my needs met the wrong and the long way around. The right thing to do was to make my peace with the fact that others decide whether to love me or not.

When my husband had a problem I used to feel bad and worry on his behalf and somehow managed to deteriorate mentally for much longer that he did. I tried to be helpful and find a positive angle that would make his problem look better. Contrary to my expectations that appeared to annoy him.

For one, it was unnecessary, because my husband wasn't expecting me to solve his problems. What he wanted was to feel bad for a while until he got over it and moved on. It was his way of processing the negative feelings. And he could cope just fine without my misguided efforts to cheer him up.

Once in a while we all need help to cope, and this is the time to lean on your partner. Most mentally healthy people do not expect others to make them feel better on a daily basis. They have their own coping mechanisms. In time I learned not to try so hard, and it was an improvement. I learned to ask for help when I needed it and that helped the relationship as well.

...

There was another thing that was bad about not having borders in a relationship. Occasionally I had the need to push him away because that state of constantly losing myself became too much and I became overwhelmed and angry.

And something even worse that that – I was feeling relief when his behaviour was thoughtless and hurtful. It was so much easier to keep borders when he was the bad guy. Nothing could get me faster into the right state of mind and into my own head.

Needless to say, it was not the way to sustain a healthy relationship – feeling close to someone should not feel like a trap.

Another example:

When I had the flu I got on with the housework and the shopping as usual. This is how it was until I realised I was putting up with a great deal of discomfort to do things like go to the shops and do the housework. This was a very unnecessary stress, and one day I asked my husband to do the shopping instead. He was a bit surprised but he got out and did the shopping. The next time I was sick he offered to do it because he knew it this was the right thing to do.

Why did I even have to ask him, you wonder? Because, given the chance, all people naturally do what is more convenient for them. I do not think that I am being cynical; it is a biological tendency most humans have. I used to refuse any offers of help so my husband figured he could just sit in the couch, and that's what he did. Self-care came naturally to him. When he was in pain he screamed, when he needed something he said so, but mostly he was happy as he was.

Normal people do not silently expect others to know what they need. That came from my dysfunctional family and the games played by my mother. Adults speak their minds, they communicate, and this is how it should be.

TAKING RESPONSIBILITY FOR MY RECOVERY

During our twenty years of marriage my husband has been consistently supportive of the changes I have gone through, but he was not helpful in any practical way. Doing that required knowledge and skills he did not have.

During my last breakdown I felt disconnected from the world, completely alone with my pain. Nobody felt what I was feeling or helped me understand what was happening. Not one human being. At this time I realised very clearly that people are separate, indeed, both physically and emotionally.

Finally I did find help online. Experiencing that sense of 'separation' was not entirely bad, because it could help me detach from the feelings of others. Enmeshment used to be my way of interaction for a very long time. I needed to remember this feeling when I needed to turn it off.

As a survivor I know I am not responsible for the actions and the feelings of other adults, and they are not responsible for mine. I already have all I need to give myself unconditional self-love and support if I want to thrive.

For me recovery became easier once I understood that my motivation should be self-care. Self-care is looking after your health, wellbeing and interests, and making these things a priority in your life. And that helped me understand that other people do the same, and their reactions and comments are coming from their own self-interests much more often than not.

HEALTHY NARCISSISM

We know that healthy narcissism is necessary for good mental health and for making good decisions. It is putting yourself first in the way you define yourself and perceive the world. This is narcissistic behaviour, and it is in the healthy range. Narcissism is a good protection against stress, and a good indicator one will succeed in life.

So why is this way of thinking not a narcissistic disorder? Two main reasons:

It is because putting yourself first is a decision you make and you take responsibility for. You are not using other people to get attention, or expecting others to give you value, fulfilment and happiness. Our narcissistic parents made us put them first, and it did not turn out well.

And second, unconditional self-love is a realistic love. Healthy narcissism is not about denying our limits and shortcomings. It is about embracing our value despite our human flaws. Healthy narcissism does not demand that others see and acknowledge the same things that we see and believe.

The narcissistic disorder, on the other hand, is a constant demand for acknowledgment of the distorted narcissistic reality. It is a consistent pattern of behaviour based on creating and protecting their false image.

So, putting yourself first is a healthy narcissism. Even if you are a parent, that ensures that you do not engage in enmeshment, and that you can be a confident reassuring parent and a fine example to your kids.

Most survivors understand this at an intellectual level but struggle with the learned responses, with the childhood programming. Mind you, being a parent is a very selfless job, and probably the only exemption to healthy narcissism – many parents do put their children first, and they do it for selfless reasons. I don't have children, but I do understand it is crucial that small children feel safe and loved in order to thrive.

PART III: Ways to Improve

You may have noticed a pattern emerging in this book when it comes to recovery. We already know how much is wrong with the narcissists. Now we have to face how much is wrong with us, the children of narcissists, and try to fix it.

In my case it took knowledge as well as honesty. Some things are easy to miss because I was so used to being the way I was that I could not see the problems. I had taken on many bad traits from my narcissistic mother. I will mention some below, and what I thought I could do to cope in a better way:

PASSIVE-AGGRESSIVE BEHAVIOUR

In the past when I became angry with people I ended up withdrawing in anger and pain and stewing in silence, rather than speaking out or working on resolving the issues. It was my inability to cope rather than wanting to be a nuisance, but let's face it, no matter what the reason might be, the silent treatment is a passive-aggressive behaviour.

Angry silence is not the way to be heard, nor the way to deal with conflict. It is basically avoiding that conflict because it is way too hard on our co-dependent and dysregulated minds.

It is easy to understand why this behaviour has to change but it is not so easy to change the physiological reactions involved. The fast heartbeat, the sensation that one is on the verge of tears, the heavy feeling in the stomach – the whole body gets involved when we face conflict and we want to get away from it.

So, on the one hand we should not stew in silence but on the other hand we are not good at dealing with conflict. What do we do?

Well, there is a middle way, and I think it works well for me. It means doing your best to communicate, but not immediately.

First, and very important, every time I feel the physical symptoms I mentioned above I know I need to stop. This is my warning system going off and it means I have to wait before I do anything further. Do not answer emails, do not answer back to people. Do not make decisions. Do not answer questions. Just say 'I will get back to you later.' Or 'I need more time, let's think about it some more and talk later.'

It is always a good idea to calm down before you approach an issue. When it comes down to your loved ones, do not break communication. Simple say 'I am sorry I am overwhelmed. Can we talk about that later?' This way you are keeping the communication open but you take the time to calm down.

After that you can make a decision, and you can be sure you have given it your best level-headed effort. If you follow this simple rule you are less likely to blow up, fall to pieces or get sucked into other people's games.

Of course, you need someone willing to communicate on the other end. If they aren't, well, you cannot be reasonable with unreasonable people. Then it's a different story altogether – engage the grey rock technique, do not give information, do not show emotion, and be relentlessly polite.

JEALOUSY

The jealousy I am talking about is not very different from the jealousy that covert narcissists experience. It came from my own damaged ego and feelings of inferiority. I am talking about jealousy towards people who have great confidence, or people who seem to have it all and who have no idea of the issues I had to struggle with. Jealousy is a pretty common feeling, everyone has felt it at one time or another.

As a little girl I used to notice other little girls with long hair and pretty dresses, who looked happy and confident and had that princess-like demeanour I wanted so much to have. Each time I saw them I used to get a strong feeling of sadness and pain.

Even as an adult, this type of girl still triggered similar feelings. It was clear just by looking at them that if anyone approached them the wrong way they would scream the world down. They had the confidence to stand up for themselves, and all the other the things I wished I had – self-respect, style, beautiful hair, good families.

Before I started recovering, such encounters triggered pain and anger against the unfair world in general. It was my injured ego. And, yes, I can see the irony. This was very much what my narcissistic mother was angry about. She could not allow her daughter to have what she didn't have – authentic self-confidence and joy. This is why she had to sabotage me each time I got close.

So my jealousy was not that different but I was capable of admitting it and looking for a better way.

Acting out from my hurt gave me nothing good back. But being happy for the confident girls put me in a positive state of mind and it gave me something good in return. Girls like that were safe from abusers, and this was a good thing. I knew they would not stand for abuse either, and would not let abusers get their way.

Progressively, the more I grasped authentic unconditional self-love, the more my experiences with jealousy disappeared. Genuinely confident and genuinely self-assured people are more tolerant and less angry and confrontational. It is not hard to understand why.

Wanting what others have for yourself is perfectly fine, it is very human. But you can want those things without a sense of jealousy and discontent towards the people that have what you want. Those two things are separate concepts. Wanting more is human, but hating those who have it is a recipe for feeling bitter and resentful.

BEING TOO SENSITIVE

You will have heard this accusation when you were growing up; it was a form of gaslighting that narcissistic parents used to shift the blame. It was never anything *they* had said or done, it was *your* fault for being too sensitive.

And guess what, we are too sensitive. We became that way. After years of abuse we ended up overreacting to all attacks, real and perceived. Nothing strange about that.

Now we have to look at what the real cost of being too sensitive is in our new lives.

Being sensitive is not necessarily bad, because our gut reactions can keep us safe. Being too sensitive is bad when we start losing opportunities and discard good people out of fear.

As a child of a narcissist you probably identify with the feeling that you are supposed to be judged but you are not allowed to judge others. This is a very child-like position to be in. It comes with being constantly criticised but not learning how to judge others.

Another sign of narcissistic abuse is not having a clear picture of what our fellow humans are like.

For example, until recently, and very much like a child, I found myself surprised when I heard people I liked talk about their friends and family behind their backs. People are far from perfect but I was so busy thinking about my own faults that I failed to notice that. I had to learn to let the small 'crimes' go because even the loveliest of people have moments when they behave badly. The key word is 'moments', of course.

The advice I can give is: stay with the people who are mostly good, and stay away from the mostly bad. Pretty simple.

Why am I talking about something so obvious? Because I know from personal experience that the reactiveness of people with C-PTSD issues and a history of abuse is off the charts. We are adults in body but we are still growing up, for the reasons I have mentioned many times before.

I thought I stopped being naïve when I started dealing with my family of origin and other toxic people. Yet I was still looking for that place where bad things and bad people did not exist. I wanted to be in an environment free of bad people and negative experiences. It is not very likely that this exists, is it?

And guess what, now I can see a bright side – we don't have to be perfect, because no one is. Claim your birthright to mess things up. Making mistakes is what happens daily. Good and bad are on a scale, just aim for less bad and more good.

And talking of scales, trauma is a common occurrence and many people carry trauma, but with some it is way up the scale and with some it is noticeable only on occasions.

The human condition is inclusive of prejudice. The high-flyers do not like the careful people. The indecisive think if you take risks you deserve any disaster you get, and everyone thinks the grass is always greener on the other side of the fence.

Which brings me to a very important point:

In general, your success rubs people up the wrong way. I have personal experience with this, and you probably have as well.

If you manage to change your core beliefs, people will not automatically be happy for you. Quite the opposite. This is why it should be very clear throughout your recovery that you are doing it for your own sake and your opinion on the subject should be the only one that matters.

This was an issue the online community prepared me for and I am grateful for that because it saved me a pile of grief. Here is what I am talking about:

PEOPLE DO NOT LIKE IT WHEN YOU CHANGE

With recovery comes change, and the change in you will not make people like you more. Not at first. They might respect you more but any significant change makes people nervous. In truth, the reason you changed had to do with you and it is supposed to benefit you, not them. If you are suddenly doing better, people around you will not like it because it changes their position in the relationship.

I used to be a 'safe' person and I actively tried not to stand out in any way, and you know why. Writing a book, for example. People who were very kind to me when I was unwell were not comfortable with it.

It did hurt but I had the knowledge and the tools to cope. I am grateful for that because this could have become a major setback on my way to recovery. Being snubbed by the very people who were good to you can be very discouraging, as you can imagine. And very painful, because survivors of narcissistic abuse are still sensitive and reactive. You may already have had similar experiences, and if you have not, it is likely to happen.

Why is that? you may wonder.

Most people want to make changes to some aspects of their lives but this is not at all easy. We were driven by the necessity to change, by the pain we were in. Well, I know I started recovery only after the pain became overwhelming and I had to do something in order to stay alive.

Change includes the risk of failure and even more emotional pain and discomfort. It is not easy, and we should appreciate and celebrate the progress we make. The people who value you will accept the new you, the others you don't care about.

Reading the accounts of survivors helped me prepare for most issues that come with recovery from co-dependency. I just carried on and eventually things got better. Which brings me to yet another question:

HOW TO MEASURE RECOVERY?

Recovery is being better than you were a day, a month, or a year before. Getting better is measured by less anxiety, less fog and fear, and more joy in life.

This is a scale as well. On occasions I had bad days and I used to worry I wasn't making any progress, but in general I was becoming a healthier person.

A good measurement of how you are is how you take care of yourself. I started taking better care of my cracked heels, cut my nails, made an effort to make my mood better. When you are in a bad place you neglect all that, and not because you don't have the time or the ability to do it. It just drops as a priority because you are busy fending off demons in your head.

I started trying new things like new styles of shoes and clothes. I tried eating new kinds of food and going to different places. Small but important things.

Another indicator is finding what gives you purpose and satisfaction. Many survivors find a calling in the mental health professions. And some of us just put more effort into learning about mental health. This is how I came to learn about the next issues I am going to share with you.

SHIFTING THE STORY

Shifting the story is redefining how we think of ourselves.

So far we have understood that we were not the bad one in the family but the product of that dysfunctional family. We were the scapegoat that was meant to carry the shame of the family.

As children we could not escape the abuse. Emotional imprinting – this is the term psychologists use to explain the effects of the behaviour of the caregivers. It means that when something is learned at an early age and in an emotional way, it is difficult to overcome.

But not impossible.

HOW DO WE CHANGE OUR STORY?

Remember how the narcissist changed the story on us by making our main characteristics undesirable, by minimising our achievements and by not letting us forget our mistakes. They found the bad in the good, and chose to devalue us for their gain.

Now we have to reverse that and choose to value and praise who we are. This is the new story: We like our main character and physical features, appreciate our uniqueness and intuition, and love who we are just because we exist. We unconditionally support our right to make mistakes, to feel, and to be flawed.

We accept and honour who we are, and this is why our worth cannot be questioned or taken for granted by others. We are mentally self-sufficient, and emotionally independent. We are enough, and this ensures we are in good company whatever happens next.

HOW DO I IDENTIFY MYSELF?

As a child I identified myself as not being attractive enough or smart enough, but being well-behaved and good at school.

I did not identify myself with being able to make decisions, or being a leader, or being confident, or easy-going, or successful in life. I was raised to be a compliant caretaker and pleaser, by parents who wanted to have a strong advantage over me for life.

Now I identify myself with survival, wisdom, knowledge and value, and with a quiet determination to take care of myself, especially my mental health. My long history of mental illness makes me who I am now. I love the person I have become.

For those of you who feel these words resonate with your internal state, that's great.

And for those of you who are not there yet, those words might evoke a tightness in your stomach and a funny sensation around the jaw – a sense of disbelief was triggered. This is a bitter feeling, a mix of disappointment and anger, as if someone is offering you something you can not possibly have.

Do not despair. I did feel that way for a very long time. The effects of the healing process accumulate over the years, and the shift will happen one day. For now just focus on getting better each day.

NO LONGER IDENTIFYING WITH THE FAMILY OF ORIGIN

An important part of shifting the story is to no longer identify as a part of the family of origin.

Something happened to me quite recently, as I was finishing this book:

As it turned out I was not out of reach and my family of origin contacted my husband through a work-related site he could not block individual users from. My parents used this to send the message that my brother had died. This was the entire message, nothing further.

The first question in my mind, as you can imagine, was: 'What? What happened?' Of course this information was not included in the message.

There was a reason behind the anger I felt all those years and it was to prepare me for moments like this. I was ready. I had never felt more awake and present in my body, more focused and determined to keep no contact.

My brother was four years older than I. He was the only person I cared for from my family of origin, because of the way we were both affected by the toxic atmosphere in the family. He became reclusive and kept the rest of the family out of his business, including me. He managed to do this as a teenager, while I became a people-pleaser and stayed under the influence of my narcissistic mother way into my adulthood.

My brother was very clever, he had a degree in astrophysics and mathematics. As I said, he became very reclusive, keeping his social life and business private, and staying in his room most of the time. He never moved out of my grandfather's apartment. For years I thought he stayed there because he could not afford to leave. I was vaguely worried about him while wrapped in my own pain and struggles, until I came across his profile online and found a list of his achievements as an author and as a translator of books from several languages. He had written articles and essays in different publications. He had written a series of science-fiction novels. My clever brother, I believe he found a way to be who he wanted to be and do what he wanted to do.

The last time I saw him was eighteen years ago. He was forty-nine when he died, and I do not know how or why.

For a while the news of his death brought on a familiar sinking feeling in my stomach – I was feeling responsible for not staying in touch, but I had to accept that it would have been hard to stay in touch with someone who did not want to stay in touch with me. Remembering him with love and respect was all I could do.

And, as a survivor, I could look back and reflect on how long I carried the family's dysfunction. Growing up I felt I was supposed to take the tension and make the family whole. It was impossible, and the burden crashed me.

This burden, however, was no longer on me. As a survivor I knew I had to stay away. The 'good' me, who felt duty-bound to take on whatever was happening, no longer existed. I kept no contact as if my life depended on it, because it did. No contact was not a game, it was a decision I made to save my life. And the only regret I have is that I did not do it much earlier.

You may have heard other survivors and thrivers say the same thing, in fact you may be one of them.

Or you may be one of the exceptions who managed recovery while maintaining low contact. I am not discarding this possibility, but in this case my story and experiences might not be relevant to your situation. The point of choosing either no contact or low contact is that the victims of abuse make a decision that is right for them.

Keeping no contact was the right thing for me to do because as time passed I felt much stronger and I felt I was a separate person with a separate identity. The childhood enmeshment and trauma bond were definitely fading away.

WHAT IS IDENTITY

Identity is not some strange substance we have to acquire. It is who we already are – the past, the present, our memories, feelings, knowledge. The sum of our experiences. The better you know who you are, the stronger your identity is.

There is plenty of advice out there about uncovering your true identity. It is about looking inside, in your heart-of-hearts, and understanding what makes you happy and motivated and what does not. Then it is about trying to do more of what makes you happy.

Sounds pretty straightforward. And as we become more able to recall memories from the past, we should make an effort to recall the good memories as well as the bad. Start thinking about it and see what will surface.

I remembered my favourite books and the things that took a hold of my imagination as a child and filled me with energy: playing in my grandfather's garden, frog ponds, collecting autumn leaves, the smell of grass, climbing trees as a child, or lying between the raspberry bushes. I remembered when my brother and I pretended to be explorers in the jungle, travelling down a river on the upturned coffee table, armed with umbrellas to fight off hippos and crocodiles.

Such memories might be few and far between but they are very valuable because they have what you want to reconnect with. I could recall happy moments alone: The first snow and being the first to walk outside in it. Jumping on the bed to music. Running around excitedly with my classmates because someone made up a story about seeing a leopard. Or playing volleyball very well one time. Just moments I felt full of life and energy.

I even remembered good times with my mother. She was quite nice when she was getting the devoted attention of a small child. And this is why, of course, she got away with her abusive behaviour for so long.

These happy memories might far between, but once you regain access you will find more.

PART IV: The Issue of Pride

Some time ago I was walking down a road near my house. The ground was wet and I slipped in some mud and fell on my bum like a sack of potatoes. The bitterness I felt was instant, and it was not about getting some mud on my clothes, or being hurt, because I wasn't. It was the 'You idiot!' reaction. My pride was hurt even though there was no one around to see me.

As I mentioned, so far I had managed to deal with my harsh inner critic and pretty much managed to stop the self-blame and self-abuse. Yet there was something else that was causing similar damage without me realising it. Once I came across the issue of pride, I recognised it was a problem for me.

WHAT IS PRIDE?

Pride is formed very early on. Small kids have pride, it's about self-awareness and measuring up. When the pride of small children is hurt they cry, it is the only thing they can do at this stage. It is up to the parent to help them cope with disappointments, criticism and with the fallout of their mistakes, as well as with the judgement of other people. Dysfunctional parents shame their children for crying and shut them up that way. The children do not learn how to cope.

Children have an instinctive need for positive regard. The good enough parents know that, and they are tuned to the emotions of the toddler and help them develop. Narcissistic parents starve their children of validation. They are like needy toddlers themselves in that respect.

Pride can be a good thing when it becomes a positive driving force. Ideally the pride of being good at something should be balanced with acceptance of one's faults as well as the ability to handle rejection.

Pride can also be a very bad thing. Pride is not unconditional love, it is the opposite of that, and it has the potential to cause harm. The danger of hurting your pride can stop you from doing things in life – being afraid to fall down, figuratively and literally, because you will look like a fool and people will laugh at you and strip down another layer of your soul.

Well, if you have experienced this fear, much it came from the narcissistic parent doing exactly that – mocking and criticising you for failing.

The question is, how do we fix this issue now?

The issue of pride sounds rather like the issue of toxic shame. Yet it is slightly different. Shame is worse, as in my opinion it is very actively corrosive. Pride helps the toxic shame. Not unlike like being 'good', it is a pushbutton and a reason why the narcissistic abuse works.

The explanation goes back to the question of why the narcissistic abuse worked so well even after we were no longer children. Co-dependents have been conditioned to be manipulated regardless of what is happening. I was attacked for my lack of abilities even when I had a high-paid job. The toxicity of the abuse increased because there was more to be tarnished before I was put back in my place.

And the reason the abuse worked was in my own head and not about what was happening in reality. My narcissistic mother could put me down because her digs caused me pain, not because they were a true representation of my character or circumstances.

My misguided pride was a pushbutton that worked to bring me down, not because I was a failure, but because I was called a failure. It was not about my abilities but about my worth, which was dependent on what I was told I was worth.

Pride is a need to be seen and judged as worthy by others. I had a childlike inability to cope with my pride. I cried instead of ignoring the unfair criticism thrown at me. My pride was trying to stop that painful criticism but doing exactly the opposite – giving it power.

It does make sense. Without the need to be seen as good, being called bad unjustly would not bother me, would it?

CHILDREN OF NARCISSISTS AND PRIDE

As a child I was only praised for good behaviour. My value was linked to pleasing my parents, and that defined me. If I got a bad grade I was upset because my mother would be displeased. My pride, the ego template of who I was as a child, was in being someone at the top of the class. This is why my mother could bring me down just by suggesting I was failing. My pride was hurt and my ego was holding on to the 'good girl' image for dear life.

Being the top of the class, however, does not translate well in real life, where you need heaps of confidence and authenticity to succeed and be happy.

You have probably heard the saying that nobody can hurt you if you don't let them. It was true enough. The hurt produced was inside of me and I was feeling the pain as a result. My misguided pride made me susceptible to emotional abuse.

SHAME-BASED PRIDE

Pride can potentially make rebellious children stand up to the putdowns of the abusers. For co-dependents pride does some of this – it rebels. This is what happens next – the hurt pride wants to prove the narcissist wrong by becoming an even better achiever and pleaser. It is a trap.

The abuser attacks us with an insinuation that we are weak or stupid, diminishing us in some way. We defend ourselves despite the fact the accusation was not true to start with. The abusers have already won because we feel driven to defend our broken ego. The moment we feel compelled to defend ourselves we give in to the accusations.

Being defensive is a co-dependent trait. Having the need to defend ourselves puts us automatically in the position of a victim. This is what bullies use to pick their targets.

Getting a hold over our pride is getting a hold over the need to be seen in a certain way by others. We do not have to defend ourselves if we have done nothing wrong.

HOW TO DEAL WITH PRIDE

If you identify with this issue, below is how I approached it:

I handled it the same way I did the critical voice and the flashbacks: identify it, face it, go through it, and come out the other side. I found logic and reason work because pride seems to be more of a frontal lobe issue rather than a C-PTSD issue.

How to stop the need to defend yourself? There is a trick to it. Do not use the reasoning: 'It does not matter what they think, because I know I am smart and clever.' This is just defending yourself to yourself.

Try the opposite. Think: 'I exist, and this is the reason I am enough. Nobody is allowed to make me feel bad. Clever or stupid, good looking or ugly, I love myself unconditionally, and I can thrive no matter what.' This works much better.

By removing the pressure you remove the elements of pride and the need to defend yourself against specific accusations. The decision about who you are is yours. And the decision to love yourself is yours.

This is the meaning of 'unconditional'. Looks and brains are what you are born with, more or less. Self-love is entirely up to you; no other has to be involved in the decision of how to feel about yourself.

Here is one example of having to deal with my pride:

At one stage I had a well-paid job in a big organization. As a child of a narcissist I tried hard to please everyone. I did well and got excellent appraisals but never a promotion. After years I was in the same position while people I had helped passed me left and right. Eventually I started to feel used and unhappy and began to unravel.

Years later I met someone from work and that triggered an old unresolved pain that was still lodged inside. My colleagues had carried on with their careers while I nosedived in the dirt with a major depression. I was exhausted, disillusioned and frustrated. The encounter made me instantly feel a bitter pain, and the cause of it was my pride. I was supposed to be the one at the 'top of the class'.

My pride needed me to be perceived as successful because I had the need to be seen in a certain way. I behaved not unlike a narcissist with a needy ego, you may have noticed. Hurt pride is a trap for the narcissists as well but their need to be special is so great they irately and shamelessly repel anything that threatens their false image rather than wince and twitch as the co-dependents do.

The sickness of the narcissists' and the co-dependents' egos do have some common elements because both are personality disorders. So it was my own pride that was causing problems for me. Pride comes from the need for validation, and kids need that. It seemed I did not quite manage to grow out of this need.

Luckily I knew I had to resolve this reaction with compassion and acceptance. The pain came from the fact I had failed to have a career and that proved that my narcissistic mother was right from the very start – I was not capable of one.

Logically, of course, I knew that I was good enough to do the job, but I unravelled in fear, self-sabotage and insecurity, because I was mentally unwell. I had to face it, I had been mentally unwell most of my life and I had been through several major depressive episodes. It started in my childhood and got progressively worse. There were times I was so ill I wasn't sure how I made it through, yet my pride insisted that I should still be the one at the 'top of the class'.

Accepting my history of depression gave me such peace of mind. I could not have done better without getting better, without dealing with my personality disorder. The next step was to make this knowledge a comfortable and important part of my identity.

And although the encounter with my ex-colleague hit me hard at first, in a few hours I had processed my misery and I was on the other side. My outlook had shifted.

Later, I figured that my pride had been a problem for a very long time. It was the reason I blamed myself for failing to understand the games my narcissistic mother was playing. My pride was arrogant; it demanded that I was stupid for being a victim and I should have known better. My pride was definitely not a friend of mine.

It turned out that, for me, a critical part of coping better was accepting my mental health history and making that a comfortable part of who I was. I had gained a lot of knowledge and skills, and dealing with my co-dependent pride was part of the recovery process.

PART V: How to Cope Better in Society

As I mentioned in the first book, there is no point trying to explain the damage done by your narcissistic parent to people who have not experienced such abuse. Especially if you are in a fragile state.

But having said that, even as a survivor I needed to express what I had been through, to put it into words for my own sake. Expressing it clearly could help me deconstruct it in a comprehensive manner and deal with it better. This is not an easy task.

If someone says 'What are you complaining about? Nobody burned you with cigarettes', it is hard to argue with that, especially if the person saying it was burned with cigarettes as a child.

It is hard to compare, and hard to explain – the closest I can think of is that the narcissistic abuse makes the victims hate who they are so much they burn themselves with cigarettes metaphorically. Psychological and emotional abuse cause a great amount of pain which drives the victim's irrational and self-destructive behaviour.

PHYSICAL vs EMOTIONAL ABUSE

With physical abuse the children are a convenient outlet for their parents' rage. The reasons for this could be unresolved trauma, need for control, anger issues, personality disorders.

The reasons for emotional abuse are not that different. What is different, however, is that the covert abusers want to look good in society, or at least they want to avoid the judgement of society. They are too afraid or too crafty to be seen as abusers.

A good analogy would be child molesters who are married with children and have a good reputation in society. They don't target their own family, but the vulnerable, damaged, already primed-for-abuse children who nobody would believe. Some get caught, but many do not.

Covert abusers intentionally put up a good façade in public. For the victims, emotional abuse is like taking poison each day, but nobody can tell this is happening. The children start to behave irrationally but society assumes they are just weird children. There is no physical way to tell what the parents are doing behind closed doors, or to make them behave differently.

The public image of covert narcissists is that of respectability and conformity, and constant self-promotion as being good parents. Nobody gets to see that they demean their children, show disgust, aggression and spite towards them, and even take pleasure in their pain.

The emotional abuse is always present with the physical, of course. The helplessness, the betrayal of those who are supposed to care, the humiliation of not being able to defend yourself – those are the exact same feelings the covert narcissist causes without the physical pain. The abuse targets the mental state of the victims and their core beliefs.

NARCISSISTIC ABUSE AGAINST SMALL CHILDREN

This, I think, should be in a separate category, and it has to do specifically with covert narcissists.

Many years ago I witnessed a scene where a mother had locked her toddler out of the house. He was alone in the dark, cold backyard and he was screaming with such terror his voice was failing, begging his mommy to let him in.

Even then, still very much in the thick of the co-dependent fog, I recognised what the mother was doing and why.

Whatever the toddler had done, it did not amount to having to experience such terror. What the mother wanted was to purposefully make him experience abandonment and fear of losing his mother, which would stay with him for the rest of his life.

Terrifying small children is easy. The mother is big and strong and almighty, and very much in a position to physically handle children. This kind of fear-based discipline is not against the law, it does not leave marks on the child, and it gets what the narcissistic parent wants – obedient children who keep mommy happy and are terrified of abandonment without even knowing why.

Covert narcissists have no empathy, they do this again and again, punishing every perceived 'rebellion' with abandonment and isolation. This is why the fight instinct does not activate in some victims of narcissistic abuse, and they let their parent damage them for decades.

Covert narcissists use the time when children are small because they know they will not be able to do this once the child is older and still maintain the image of the good parent in front of society. Later they can control and manipulate just by pushing the buttons they created.

...

What is the point of me going back to this? Observing what happened to us as children from a detached viewpoint gives us a perspective about humanity, and it will help us understand how we fit into a society that allows for such abuse.

I will briefly mention some other aspects of early childhood abuse before we get to the topic of what to do about the lack of understanding or justice:

EMOTIONAL NEGLECT

Emotional neglect is even harder to explain.

I try to use words like 'always' and 'never' with care because they are extreme and the everyday life is not that clearly polarised. I will say, however, that I have not been able to think of one clear case when my parents said something positive or uplifting about who I was. Not one. The negative they pointed out constantly.

This was an extreme one-sided parental behaviour, and the damage done as a result was severe. Not giving a child any positive feedback about who they are is abuse. It is starving them of positive regard and validation.

As a survivor I understand that, and you probably understand that, but I do not expect anyone else to do so.

THE DUNEDIN STUDY

Dunedin is a town in New Zealand. The Dunedin Study is a longitudinal detailed study of human health, development and behaviour. It is the gold standard for such studies, following closely more than a 1000 people for 45 years. The award-winning documentary *Predict My Future: The Science of Us* is based on this ongoing study.

The study covers a wide area of human behaviour. The area I will mention is childhood adversity and the life outcomes for children growing up in abusive environments. What the study found was that the first six years were a good indicator of the future lives of the individuals participating. Children shaped by violence ended up in and out of prison.

The conclusion of the study was that early intervention is critical, and helping such children is possible only early on before too much damage is done to them. 'Early on', in the context of the study, means during the early character-forming years.

Taking children from their parents, however, is sacrilegious. With society still struggling to digest the outcome of the obvious types of abuse, any helpful documentaries about covert emotional abuse are long way off.

This is not new information but now there is strong scientific research to back it. The first years in the development of children are critical. A child's personality and outlooks are formed at an early age in the family, and what they learn back then has a powerful impact on their lives. Much like in the earlier umbrella story I mentioned, the effects of such abuse are hard to change.

I am not saying this to discourage you. On the contrary. Remember the progress we have made? It was such a hard thing to do but we made it to the survivor stage. Don't stop. Keep on using acceptance, compassion and self-love. Every effort counts. And keep in mind that we are doing this for our benefit, so listen to your own intuition and you decide what is good for you.

Society is not going to change in a hurry, but we can change.

THE WORST ASPECT OF COVERT NARCISSISTIC ABUSE

Children of narcissists know the worst consequence of the abuse is that we abandon ourselves, our side of the story, our values, borders and intuition, and we give control of our souls to external forces.

This is a fair statement, I believe, but it is only understood by those who have experienced narcissistic abuse in one form or another.

Example:

At one stage my husband had a toxic boss who devalued him and played narcissistic power games. In no time my husband turned into an angry, reactive, broken person. Everyone who has had a close encounter with toxic people knows how it feels. Luckily his boss was forced to leave and that was over with.

After that I told my husband to imagine having such a toxic person as a parent, and he understood. For the first time I felt he knew what I meant. Yet I still don't think he fully understood how overwhelming such toxicity is to a child, and how it nearly drove me to suicide.

Now, the big question:

WHAT DO WE DO ABOUT COVERT EMOTIONAL ABUSE?

So, we know what it is. But what do we do about it? How do we get justice?

Fairness does not exist in nature. Many people suffer injustice, bad things happen all the time in this very imperfect world. One has to accept that many things are not fair. Accidents and diseases, for example. I saw a newspaper headline which said: 'Newborns perish in a hospital fire.' One cannot possibly find any fairness in that.

So, here we are. Fairness is a social construct, and it is there to maintain order and to protect the population from murderers, sexual predators and such. It has not yet extended to children of emotionally abusive parents.

While it is becoming acceptable to maintain no contact with a parent, and the effects of bad parenting are talked about, the emotional abuse issues have not reached the courts in any way that I know of.

Abuse stories, in general, make people uncomfortable. Fair enough. I am not sure I want to take on the burdens and the negative experiences of others. But sexual and physical abuse against children is strongly condemned, while covert emotional abuse is not. Covert abusers are not likely to face justice from society, and we have to deal with that injustice in the best way we can.

This is not a unique situation. In the past, generations have been affected by abuse without even having that acknowledged. Physical abuse was not only acceptable but widespread. Abuse has always been a part of human nature and part of the workings of the damaged human ego.

In the developing world, where life is hard and there is a lack of security, the children become a resource. In these cases some parents cannibalise the autonomy and wellbeing of their children to get what is needed for their own wellbeing. But even in this context some parents create a relationship with their children based on closeness and empathy, while others use fear and shame.

Progress comes when the mindset of a generation changes. Self-esteem is a relatively new concept. Treating children well creates better people – not such a difficult concept to understand.

Why am I going on about issues that I am not an expert in? Because I have experienced them, they are part of my story, and probably part of yours. And because I am getting to the question of how to deal with the unfairness and with the lack of justice for emotional abuse victims, in a helpful manner.

EMOTIONAL ABUSE AND OBSESSION WITH FAIRNESS

I asked myself why I found it so hard to let go of my need for fairness. Why did I get so upset when things were not fair, for me and for other victims? I think the answer is because of the way the very idea of good and bad gets twisted when it comes to covert narcissistic mothers. The very idea of the mother as being selfless and loving, in contrast to the reality of the abuse we grew up with. This was the nasty trick played on us.

Yet we know that unfairness is everywhere. Many violent abusers get away with their crimes. What else could be behind the need for fairness?

First, there was the betrayal of trust. The abuse came from those who were supposed to teach us about things like dealing with unfairness. Mind you, sexual and physical abuse are a major betrayal of trust as well. All victims want and need justice in order to recover.

Being disregarded by society might be another reason. Explaining the abuse is a hard thing to do. But why do we have to explain it to others?

I think it is because we want to have the unfairness acknowledged in the hope that will fix us. This is not a helpful way of thinking. It might help, but acknowledging the abuse will not fix the damage done.

Let's face it, even if the whole world agrees with us, we still have to deal with the issues inside of us. First, we have to focus on getting better, then worry about justice after that.

Experiencing unfairness and overreacting to it is similar to experiencing abuse and overreacting to it, in all aspects. It is a particular trait of our disorder.

HOW TO DEAL WITH NO JUSTICE

We have to deal with it the same way we dealt with the hope that the abuser will change. And the same way we dealt with the need to prove ourselves.

Justice may never come. We may never see the narcissist punished. This is a fact, and this is not a fair world we live in. This does not feel very good, I agree. But it is true. Instead of focusing on the lack of fairness, let's focus on recovery without fairness.

We have to stop being vulnerable children. We have our truth, and those who question our truth have to prove themselves. We do not have to experience justice to know we are right.

The answer is as before – we have to focus on us, change what we can inside of us. Fix the world afterwards, if you wish, but first let's finish the recovery process.

So, the next big question:

IS IT POSSIBLE TO THRIVE WITHOUT JUSTICE?

The answer is yes. We can thrive without justice. It comes with acquiring new mental agility and strength.

It is the same with victims of all kinds of abuse – some recover quickly, some carry the scars for decades. It depends on their mental agility. The key is not what happened but how it affected the victim, and whether they get the right help and information to cope well.

As co-dependents we were the epitome of victim. We had no skills to cope whatsoever. This has changed, however, and now we can. In a way, as we became survivors, we learned what all victims of abuse have to learn to stop being victims.

As my recovery progressed through the years, the need for justice started to fade. My need for acknowledgment by the outside world changed and I became more capable of giving myself affirmation and support.

So this is it. By relinquishing the need for justice we can thrive without it. We have to change what we need and our frame of reference. Changing ourselves is very much within our power – developing good borders, closing the wounds and becoming emotionally self-sufficient people. And this solves the problem with any future narcissistic abuse. If your ego is healthy, they have nothing to feed on. You begin to repel covert narcissists and toxic people.

This is closure, as far as I can tell.

SOCIETY'S ATTITUDE TO MENTAL HEALTH

In general the attitude of the general population to mental health has not caught up with the progress in the psychology field on depression, suicide and emotional abuse.

This is a useful topic to us, because we have to navigate society throughout our recovery without putting ourselves in danger. Remember: observe but do not absorb. I used to feel issues like this inside of me but now I can be a calm observer because my truth does not get affected easily. I know who I am and what happened to me.

The examples I will give are from New Zealand, a country that prides itself on being liberal and progressive. It has a very good record of respect for human rights and tolerance of differences. It is a country with one of the western-world's best medical care systems. Yet it has some of the highest numbers of suicides among young people. However, the medical examiners are not allowed to report the method of suicide. The media is not supposed to call it a suicide, but a 'sudden death'.

Recently the media and certain political groups have started challenging the old perceptions and started talking about mental health and death, or at least letting the affected people talk about it. Obviously not the dead – they don't get to speak for themselves – but those near to them.

There was an article in one of the most respected newspapers in the country, and I am going to use it without too many specific details, to illustrate a point.

Example:

A high school boy had killed himself, and his mother had taken the opportunity to talk about suicide publically. In it she said that her son was a good student and a well-behaved boy, and that he had no problems whatsoever. She blamed the death on the friends he made behind her back.

Her son had betrayed her, she said in the article, because he started staying out late with friends. She proceeded to say how he kissed her the very night he died, said good night, and went to bed as if there was nothing out of the ordinary.

As a survivor of abuse I could see clearly the characteristics of a dysfunctional family in this article. To start with, there is no such thing as a person with no problems. Everyone has problems. Everyone. Small kids, teenagers and adults. Problems are an everyday occurrence. Every human being deals with problems on a daily basis. There are, however, children who are not allowed to have problems, and this happens when the parents are in denial or do not wish to deal with this fact.

Another one was the 'betrayal' mentioned in the article. The son's attempts at becoming a teenager and having friends were about the mother. Betrayal? The whole article was about the mother.

Those were just two of the most disturbing signs of dysfunction. The 'perfect' son who was not allowed to have problems and clearly was not allowed to enter adolescence as other teenagers were. Maybe I was reading my story into it, but the clues were there and any psychologist or therapist could see them.

Yet nobody would dare speak up.

The mother was covered by the social convention that she was a grieving mother who had lost her son. Did she have a personality disorder? Maybe. Maybe she grew up in a dysfunctional home and she did not know better.

Isn't it funny how one can find excuses for emotional abuse but the same excuses do not work for sexual and physical abuse?

This one article, as with most of the others, was not helpful because it did not offer solutions. It did offer contact numbers at the end, as do all articles involving suicide.

The article itself, in my opinion, had no value to anyone but the mother who voiced her dismay and disapproval that her son killed himself. This is my opinion, of course, but this book is about my outlook as a survivor of covert emotional abuse.

…

In another article, a ten-year-old girl killed herself. Afterwards the authorities discovered she had been bullied at school and this was the likely reason for her suicide.

Reading this I could not help wondering why this ten-year-old did not go to her parents for help but killed herself instead? Kids are supposed to look up to their parents for help and support. She did not.

Of course I am using my own story as a measuring stick, but I believe this is a valid question. Is it possible that going to her parents would have been worse than facing the bullies at school? Not in an obvious, violent way, but in a demeaning, suffocating, soul-crushing way? There is such a thing as bullies at home, and most of you probably know that. It was possible that there was nowhere safe for her.

It is possible, of course, that the parents were clueless, and most people reading the article would be compelled to feel bad for the parents without realising how much pain one must be in to actually end one's life. We will never know what really happened .

I have mentioned only two examples. Those articles were not helpful to the victims, obviously. But were they helpful to anyone?

There were other articles from parents who sounded pretty decent. They described their pain and confusion, and their grief appeared genuine. There were one or two articles by survivors of suicide attempts, describing their experiences with depression.

But none of those was written by experts, nor by survivors who had been suicidal and made a full recovery. They did not offer any solutions, just muddied the water with hints that suicide happens out of the blue and for no apparent reason.

It was like a public campaign of awareness – a cacophony of voices making lots and lots of noise. And maybe that was the whole idea, to bring the attention of the nation to the problem of suicide.

I do understand why most mental health professionals do not want to participate in newspaper campaigns, but without their input, and without answers, how can there be any positive results?

As far as I can understand, there is yet no reliable physical way to measure depression or assess the mental health of a person. And there is no definitive agreement on depression and what causes it. Possibly the condition describes a state of mind that can be a result of many things.

What can we do about this state of sanctioned confusion? We can keep on healing as best as we can. My advice is: don't try to explain what happened to you to people with no knowledge of emotional abuse or personality disorders. And remember, you cannot help people who do not want to be helped, even if they are fellow co-dependents. This is part of the self-care we need to practice.

BAD ADVICE GIVEN FOR DEPRESSION

The general advice for good health is to exercise, eat well, be positive, take care of yourself. It's all good. And if you have a serious physical illness the official advice is to seek medical help, not simply to go out and exercise to get better. Unfortunately the guidelines as to what is 'serious' when it comes to mental illness are not so clear or widely acknowledged.

I mentioned the high number of suicides in New Zealand. In an attempt to reduce this, a TV ad campaign advised people to tell someone when they are feeling depressed and suicidal. This advice very much clashes with another popular piece of advice for good mental health, which is to stay away from people who bring you down.

It is very obvious that depressed people bring others down. They are the opposite to a barrel of laughs. And it is pretty clear to anyone that most people are going prioritise their own mental health and that of their family above someone else's. Yet the 'Tell Someone' people chose to ignore this simple truth.

It felt as if the creators of this TV campaign believed they can make people be nice just by telling them to be nice. This is a very naïve and irresponsible approach.

A likely outcome is that the depressed person will be rejected, minimised, or even laughed at. The average person is not equipped to deal with mental illnesses, the same way they are not equipped to deal with diabetes or cancer.

Another thing that nobody wants to talk about is the issue of the predators out there, who prey on the vulnerability of the mentally ill. Telling such people you are depressed is the worst idea ever.

Much better advice, in my opinion, would be to talk to a medical professional. For any other illnesses the advice is to go to a health professional rather than a friend or a stranger. The chances are that you are going to get more understanding and help from them.

I did get medical help from a General Practitioner, and I believe the medication I was put on helped enough to give me the chance to work on resolving my childhood abuse issues. I stopped taking the medication when I had recovered sufficiently, and I did this under my doctor's supervision.

Having a good therapist is the best option, but finding a mental health specialist back then seemed impossible for me. I had no energy, and no knowledge or desire to do so. I did not know I had the issues I did. When the doctor asked me if I had any problems I wanted to talk about, I just started crying. Asking for help was beyond me.

Luckily I found the information I needed online, and I followed the advice of survivors who used to have the same problems and who felt the same way I did. It was a lifeline.

Now I have written this book about my own experiences. I am not a certified health professional, and you don't have to follow my advice, of course. Just consider it as one option if you feel it is the right thing for you, and if my story is similar to yours.

AT THE END OF THIS BOOK

Obviously what I feared at the start of this book was not true. The process of recovery had not halted, and I had the potential to get better.

I don't even know why I doubted that. Every single year since I went no contact with my family of origin has been better than the one before. There was no miracle cure, just different stages of the recovery process. It took time and effort but it was worth it.

This book is about the process of undoing the damage done to us by our narcissistic parents. But if you were to ask me what the most important stage, the most important discovery, the strongest reason for a change was that I had experienced, I would say it was getting that sense of unconditional self-love I have talked about in both books.

I have read widely about what others have to say about self-love. Many emphasise the description of self-love as an appreciation that comes from the actions of a person, from changes and growth, others say that you simply have to be in tune with your spirit and your soul.

I think self-love is essential to thriving, much like breathing is to staying alive. Not unlike self-worth, it is not something that changes with circumstances or with age. It is a biological necessity, like self-preservation, and it is an internal source of energy, mental strength and independence. Self-preservation is not selfish. It is a biological imperative. So is self-love. It is a driving force of life.

This sounds like a pep talk, but you know what that candle was about, that little light inside of us that dwindled but never went out – it was our inherent biological will to live. It was the sense of our innate value, and the reason we did not give up.

Now we have to embrace this self-love. It is a warm feeling of belonging, internal peace and positive regard. This is exactly what good mental health is based on – to stay well we must have a constructive and positive regard for who we are. Having that means having a strong identity and borders.

SO, WHAT NEXT?

The next step is to integrate all the versions of ourselves. It was pretty clear to me that to complete the healing process I had to accept and integrate all versions of myself into one – the small anxious child, the desperate tortured teen, the anxious unhappy adult. Sounds terrible, doesn't it? I am sure you can relate. And I am sure you know where I am going with this.

It may sound counterintuitive, but integrating these parts into a whole will make all the difference. The last part, the survivor, will take hold of the present and the rest will fall in line in the past and lose their hold over you.

All versions of you are part of you, just like I am both the person who was depressed and miserable and the one who managed to heal. I am the broken one who nearly gave up and the one who ended writing this book. Unconditional love means loving all versions of me.

Here is a question: Would you choose to forget your childhood memories? I would not, not as a survivor. The memories are what make me, and I never want to forget the lessons I have learned.

There was a time, however, when I was in so much pain I would have swapped with someone else in a heartbeat – a clear sign of an unhealthy mental state. I think any healthy person would choose to remember who they were from the start.

Integrating all parts means accepting, of course, all versions as valuable parts of us. As survivors we know how to love the child, and calm the teen, and be responsible for our own state of mind. We have done the hard work behind the process.

Complete integration occurs when the survivor takes charge and healthy reactions become automatic, and when we no longer have to think what is the right way to react or approach something. Eventually we will stop thinking about the past and start living in the present in a positive and supportive manner.

WHY WE GAINED MORE THAN WE LOST

When it comes to my own journey, the better I get the more I understand that my life used to be like trying to walk through thick syrup – I was constantly getting tangled up with the identities of others, holding myself down and trying to somehow achieve happiness by pleasing those around me.

This did not work at all.

What did work was the opposite – focusing on my everyday needs, and loving who I was as I was: imperfect, vulnerable, hurt, happy, angry, mistaken, egotistic, successful or insecure.

Why did this work? Because that is what a healthy ego is about – realistic appraisal, acceptance, self-love, a will to improve and fight abuse from others, and the desire to stay positive and make good things happen.

What is the goal of recovery? It is to have so much unconditional love you can give it away without any fear. This is when the scales have tipped towards thriving.

If you are reading this book you are probably familiar with the online community of survivors of narcissistic abuse. And you may have noticed the members who have made the journey to thriving, because they glow. This is the only way to describe it. You can plainly see they are healthier, happier, and they have this aura of peace and contentment about them that is indisputable.

And this is why I think that all the pain we went through is good in a way. We have made the journey and resolved the issues on our way. Nobody can take this away. We gained knowledge and developed immunity to the mental challenges in life. And we have the tools when it comes to handling the low points of life.

Finding out something the hard way is more appreciated, like finding freedom and enjoyment later in life. After the storm the sun comes out and the peace and quiet are so much more appreciated.

Imagine, the rest of our lives can be really good and we might just become happy old people, the kind who quietly glow because they know what life is about. Allow yourself to sit quietly and glow for no other reason but because you are alive, and that is great.

Printed in Great Britain
by Amazon